LIZA

OR, "A NEST OF NOBLES"

A NOVEL

IVAN S. TURGENEV

TRANSLATED FROM THE RUSSIAN
BY W.R.S. RALSTON

1st WORLD
LIBRARY
Literary Society

Liza

Ivan Sergeevich Turgenev

© 1st World Library, 2008
PO Box 2211
Fairfield, IA 52556
www.1stworldlibrary.com
First Edition

LCCN: 2007935396

Softcover ISBN: 978-1-4218-9343-3
Hardcover ISBN: 978-1-4218-9443-0
eBook ISBN: 978-1-4218-9243-6

Purchase *"Liza"*
as a traditional bound book at:
www.1stWorldLibrary.com/purchase.asp?ISBN=978-1-4218-9343-3

1st World Library is a literary, educational organization
dedicated to:

- Creating a free internet library of downloadable ebooks

- Hosting writing competitions and offering book publishing
scholarships.

Interested in more 1st World Library books? contact:
literacy@1stworldlibrary.com
Check us out at: www.1stworldlibrary.com

1st World Library Literary Society

Giving Back to the World

"If you want to work on the core problem, it's early school literacy."

- James Barksdale, former CEO of Netscape

"No skill is more crucial to the future of a child, or to a democratic and prosperous society, than literacy."

- Los Angeles Times

"Literacy... means far more than learning how to read and write... The aim is to transmit... knowledge and promote social participation."

- UNESCO

"Literacy is not a luxury, it is a right and a responsibility. If our world is to meet the challenges of the twenty-first century we must harness the energy and creativity of all our citizens."

- President Bill Clinton

"Parents should be encouraged to read to their children, and teachers should be equipped with all available techniques for teaching literacy, so the varying needs and capacities of individual kids can be taken into account."

- Hugh Mackay

DEDICATED TO THE AUTHOR BY HIS
FRIEND THE TRANSLATOR

PREFACE

The author of the *Dvoryanskoe Gnyezdo*, or "Nest of Nobles," of which a translation is now offered to the English reader under the title of "Liza," is a writer of whom Russia may well be proud.[A] And that, not only because he is a consummate artist,—entitled as he is to take high rank among those of European fame, so accurate is he in his portrayal of character, and so quick to seize and to fix even its most fleeting expression; so vividly does he depict by a few rapid touches the appearance of the figures whom he introduces upon his canvas, the nature of the scenes among which they move,—he has other and even higher claims than these to the respect and admiration of Russian readers. For he is a thoroughly conscientious worker; one who, amid all his dealings with fiction, has never swerved from his regard for what is real and true; one to whom his own country and his own people are very dear, but who has neither timidly bowed to the prejudices of his countrymen, nor obstinately shut his eyes to their faults.

[Footnote A: Notwithstanding the unencouraging opinion expressed by Mr. Ralston in this preface, of the probable fate of "Fathers and Children," and "Smoke," with the English public, both have been translated in America and have met with very fair success. Of course, even more may be hoped for the author's other works.]

His first prose work, the "Notes of a Sportsman" (*Zapiski Okhotnika*), a collection of sketches of country life, made a deep and lasting impression upon the minds of the educated classes in Russia, so vigorous were its attacks upon the vices of that system of slavery which was then prevalent. Those attacks had all the more weight, inasmuch as the book was by no means exclusively devoted to them. It dealt with many other subjects connected with provincial life; and the humor and the pathos and the picturesqueness with which they were treated would of themselves have been sufficient to commend it to the very favorable attention of his countrymen. But the sad pictures he drew in it, occasionally and almost as it were accidentally, of the wretched position occupied by the great masses of the people, then groaning under the weight of that yoke which has since been removed, stirred the heart of Russian society with a thrill of generous horror and sympathy; and the effect thus produced was all the more permanent inasmuch as it was attained by thoroughly legitimate means. Far from exaggerating the ills of which he wrote, or describing them in sensational and declamatory language, he treated them in a style that sometimes seemed almost cold in its reticence and freedom from passion. The various sketches of which the volume was composed appeared at intervals in a Russian magazine, called the *Contemporary (Sovremennik)*, about three-and-twenty years ago, and were read in it with avidity; but when the first edition of the collected work was exhausted, the censors refused to grant permission to the author to print a second, and so for many years the complete book was not to be obtained in Russia without great difficulty. Now that the good fight of emancipation has been fought, and the victory—thanks to the present Emperor—has been won, M. Turgenieff has every reason for looking back with pride upon that phase of the struggle; and his countrymen may well have a feeling of regard, as well as of respect, for him—the upper-classes as for one who has helped them to recognize their duty; the lower, as for a very generous supporter in their time of trouble.

M. Turgenieff has written a great number of very charming short stories, most of them having reference to Russia and Russian life; for though he has lived in Germany for many years, his thoughts, whenever he takes up his pen, almost always seem to go back to his native land. Besides these, as well as a number of critical essays, plays, and poems, he has brought out several novels, or rather novelettes, for none of them have attained to three-volume dimensions. Of these, the most remarkable are the one I have now translated, which appeared about eleven years ago, and the two somewhat polemical stories, called "Fathers and Children" (*Otsui i Dyeti*) and "Smoke" (*Duim*). The first of the three I may leave to speak for itself, merely adding that I trust that—although it appears under all the disadvantages by which even the most conscientious of translations must always be attended—it may be looked upon by English readers with somewhat of the admiration which I have long felt for the original, on account of the artistic finish of its execution, the purity of its tone, and the delicacy and the nobleness of the sentiment by which it is pervaded.

The story of "Fathers and Children" conveys a vigorous and excessively clever description of the change that has taken place of late years in the thoughts and feelings of the educated classes of Russian society One of the most interesting chapters in "Liza"—one which may be skipped by readers who care for nothing but incident in a story—describes a conversation which takes place between the hero and one of his old college friends. The sketch of the disinterested student, who has retained in mature life all the enthusiasm of his college days, is excellent, and is drawn in a very kindly spirit. But in "Fathers and Children" an exaggeration of this character is introduced, serving as a somewhat scare-crow-like embodiment of the excessively hard thoughts and very irreverent speculations in which the younger thinkers of the new school indulge. This character is developed in the story into dimensions which must be styled inordinate if considered from a purely artistic point of view; but the story ought not to be so regarded. Unfortunately for its proper appreciation among us, it cannot be judged aright, except by readers who possess a thorough knowledge of what was going on in Russia a few years ago, and who take a keen and lively interest in the subjects which were then being discussed there. To all others, many of its chapters will seem too unintelligible and wearisome, both linked together into interesting unity by the slender thread of its story, beautiful as many of its isolated passages are. The same objection may be made to "Smoke." Great spaces in that work are devoted to caricatures of certain persons and opinions of note in Russia, but utterly unknown in England—pictures which either delight or irritate the author's countrymen, according to the tendency of their social and political speculations, but which are as meaningless to the untutored English eye as a collection of "H.B."'s drawings would be to a Russian who had never studied English politics. Consequently neither of these stories is likely ever to be fully appreciated among us[A].

[Footnote A: A detailed account of both of these stories, as well as of several other works by M. Turgenieff, will be found in the number of the *North British Review* for March, 1869.]

The last novelette which M. Turgenieff has published, "The Unfortunate One" (*Neschastnaya*) is free from the drawbacks by which, as far as English readers are concerned, "Fathers and Children" and "Smoke," are attended; but it is

Ivan S. Turgenev

exceedingly sad and painful. It is said to be founded on a true story, a fact which may account for an intensity of gloom in its coloring, the darkness of which would otherwise seem almost unartistically overcharged.

Several of M. Turgenieff's works have already been translated into English. The "Notes of a Sportsman" appeared about fourteen years ago, under the title of "Russian Life in the Interior[A];" but, unfortunately, the French translation from which they were (with all due acknowledgment) rendered, was one which had been so "cooked" for the Parisian market, that M. Turgenieff himself felt bound to protest against it vigorously. It is the more unfortunate inasmuch as an admirable French translation of the work was afterwards made by M. Delaveau[B].

[Footnote A: "Russian Life in the Interior." Edited by J.D. Meiklejohn. Black, Edinburg, 1855.]

[Footnote B: "Recits d'un Chasseur." Traduits par H. Delavea, Paris, 1858.]

Still more vigorously had M. Turgenieff to protest against an English translation of "Smoke," which appeared a few months ago.

The story of "Fathers and Children" has also appeared in English[A]; but as the translation was published on the other side of the Atlantic, it has as yet served but little to make M. Turgenieff's name known among us.

[Footnote A: "Fathers and Sons." Translated from the Russian by Eugene Schuyler. New York 1867.]

The French and German translations of M. Turgenieff's works are excellent. From the French versions of M.

Delaveau, M. Xavier Marmier, M. Prosper Merimee, M. Viardot, and several others, a very good idea may be formed by the general reader of M. Turgenieffs merits. For my own part, I wish cordially to thank the French and the German translators of the *Dvoryanskoe Gnyezdo* for the assistance their versions rendered me while I was preparing the present translation of that story. The German version, by M. Paul Fuchs,[A] is wonderfully literal. The French version, by Count Sollogub and M.A. de Calonne, which originally appeared in the *Revue Contemporaine*, without being quite so close, is also very good indeed.[B]

[Footnote A: Das adelige Nest. Von I.S. Turgenieff. Aus dem Russicher ubersetzt von Paul Fuchs. Leipzig, 1862.]

[Footnote B: Une Nichee de Gentilshommes. Paris, 1862]

I, too, have kept as closely as I possibly could to the original. Indeed, the first draft of the translation was absolutely literal, regardless of style or even idiom. While in that state, it was revised by the Russian friend who assisted me in my translation of Krilofs Fables—M. Alexander Onegine—and to his painstaking kindness I am greatly indebted for the hope I venture to entertain that I have not "traduced" the author I have undertaken to translate. It may be as well to state that in the few passages in which my version differs designedly from the ordinary text of the original, I have followed the alterations which M. Turgenieff made with his own hand in the copy of the story on which I worked, and the title of the story has been altered to its present form with his consent.

I may as well observe also, that while I have inserted notes where I thought their presence unavoidable, I have abstained as much as possible from diverting the reader's attention from the story by obtrusive asterisks, referring to what might

Ivan S. Turgenev

seem impertinent observations at the bottom of the page. The Russian forms of name I have religiously preserved, even to the extent of using such a form as Ivanich, as well as Ivanovich, when it is employed by the author.

INNER TEMPLE, June 1, 1869.

I

A beautiful spring day was drawing to a close. High aloft in the clear sky floated small rosy clouds, which seemed never to drift past, but to be slowly absorbed into the blue depths beyond.

At an open window, in a handsome mansion situated in one of the outlying streets of O., the chief town of the government of that name—it was in the year 1842—there were sitting two ladies, the one about fifty years old, the other an old woman of seventy.

The name of the first was Maria Dmitrievna Kalitine. Her husband, who had formerly occupied the post of Provincial Procurator, and who was well known in his day as a good man of business—a man of bilious temperament, confident, resolute, and enterprising—had been dead ten years. He had received a good education, and had studied at the university, but as the family from which he sprang was a poor one, he had early recognized the necessity of making a career for himself and of gaining money.

Maria Dmitrievna married him for love. He was good-looking, he had plenty of sense, and, when he liked, he could be very agreeable. Maria Dmitrievna, whose maiden name was Pestof, lost her parents while she was still a child. She spent several years in an Institute at Moscow, and then went to live with her brother and one of her aunts at Pokrovskoe, a family estate situated fifteen versts from O. Soon afterwards her brother was called away on duty to St. Petersburgh, and, until a sudden death put an end to his career, he kept his aunt and sister with only just enough for them to live upon. Maria Dmitrievna inherited Pokrovskoe, but she did not long reside there. In the second year of her marriage with Kalitine, who had succeeded at the end of a few days in gaining her affections, Pokrovskoe was exchanged for another estate— one of much greater intrinsic value, but unattractive in appearance, and not provided with a mansion. At the same time Kalitine purchased a house in the town of O., and there he and his wife permanently established themselves. A large garden was attached to it, extending in one direction to the fields outside the town, "so that," Kalitine, who was by no means an admirer of rural tranquillity, used to say, "there is no reason why we should go dragging ourselves off into the country." Maria Dmitrievna often secretly regretted her beautiful Pokrovskoe, with its joyous brook, its sweeping meadows, and its verdant woods, but she never opposed her husband in any thing, having the highest respect for his judgment and his knowledge of the world. And when he died, after fifteen years of married life, leaving behind him a son and two daughters, Maria Dmitrievna had grown so accustomed to her house and to a town life, that she had no inclination to change her residence.

In her youth Maria Dmitrievna had enjoyed the reputation of being a pretty blonde, and even in her fiftieth year her features were not unattractive, though they had lost somewhat of their fineness and delicacy. She was naturally sensitive and impressionable, rather than actually goodhearted, and even in her years of maturity she continued to behave in the manner peculiar to "Institute girls;" she denied herself no indulgence, she was easily put out of temper, and

Ivan S. Turgenev

she would even burst into tears if her habits were interfered with. On the other hand, she was gracious and affable when all her wishes were fulfilled, and when nobody opposed her in any thing. Her house was the pleasantest in the town; and she had a handsome income, the greater part of which was derived from her late husband's earnings, and the rest from her own property. Her two daughters lived with her; her son was being educated in one of the best of the crown establishments at St. Petersburgh.

The old lady who was sitting at the window with Maria Dmitrievna was her father's sister, the aunt with whom she had formerly spent so many lonely years at Pokrovskoe. Her name was Marfa Timofeevna Pestof. She was looked upon as an original, being a woman of an independent character, who bluntly told the truth to every one, and who, although her means were very small, behaved in society just as she would have done had she been rolling in wealth. She never could abide the late Kalitine, and as soon as her niece married him she retired to her own modest little property, where she spent ten whole years in a peasant's smoky hut. Maria Dmitrievna was rather afraid of her. Small in stature, with black hair, a sharp nose, and eyes which even in old age were still keen, Marfa Timofeevna walked briskly, held herself bolt upright, and spoke quickly but distinctly, and with a loud, high-pitched voice. She always wore a white cap, and a white *kofta*[A] always formed part of her dress.

[Footnote A: A sort of jacket.]

"What is the matter?" she suddenly asked. "What are you sighing about?"

"Nothing," replied Maria Dmitrievna. "What lovely clouds!"

"You are sorry for them, I suppose?"

Maria Dmitrievna made no reply.

"Why doesn't Gedeonovsky come?" continued Marfa Timofeevna, rapidly plying her knitting needles. (She was making a long worsted scarf.) "He would have sighed with you. Perhaps he would have uttered some platitude or other."

"How unkindly you always speak of him! Sergius Petrovich is—a most respectable man."

"Respectable!" echoed the old lady reproachfully.

"And then," continued Maria Dmitrievna, "how devoted he was to my dear husband! Why, he can never think of him without emotion."

"He might well be that, considering that your husband pulled him out of the mud by the ears," growled Marfa Timofeevna, the needles moving quicker than ever under her fingers. "He looks so humble," she began anew after a time. "His head is quite grey, and yet he never opens his mouth but to lie or to slander. And, forsooth, he is a councillor of state! Ah, well, to be sure, he is a priest's son."[A]

[Footnote A: *Popovich*, or son of a pope; a not over respectful designation in Russia.]

"Who is there who is faultless, aunt? It is true that he has this weakness. Sergius Petrovich has not had a good education, I admit—he cannot speak French—but I beg leave to say that I think him exceedingly agreeable."

"Oh, yes, he fawns on you like a dog. As to his not speaking French, that's no great fault. I am not very strong in the French 'dialect' myself. It would be better if he spoke no language at all; he wouldn't tell lies then. But of course, here he is, in the very nick of time," continued Marfa Timofeevna, looking down the street. "Here comes your agreeable man, striding along. How spindle-shanked he is, to be sure—just like a stork!"

Maria Dmitrievna arranged her curls. Marfa Timofeevna looked at her with a quiet smile.

"Isn't that a grey hair I see, my dear? You should scold Pelagia. Where can her eyes be?"

"That's just like you, aunt," muttered Maria Dmitrievna, in a tone of vexation, and thrumming with her fingers on the arm of her chair.

"Sergius Petrovich Gedeonovsky!" shrilly announced a rosy-cheeked little Cossack,[A] who suddenly appeared at the door.

[Footnote A: A page attired in a sort of Cossack dress.]

II

A tall man came into the room, wearing a good enough coat, rather short trousers, thick grey gloves, and two cravats—a black one outside, a white one underneath. Every thing belonging to him was suggestive of propriety and decorum, from his well-proportioned face, with locks carefully smoothed down over the temples, to his heelless and never-creaking boots. He bowed first to the mistress of the house, then to Marfa Timofeevna, and afterwards, having slowly taken off his gloves, he approached Maria Dmitrievna and respectfully kissed her hand twice. After that he leisurely subsided into an easy-chair, and asked, as he smilingly rubbed together the tips of his fingers—

"Is Elizaveta quite well?"

"Yes," replied Maria Dmitrievna, "she is in the garden."

"And Elena Mikhailovna?"

"Lenochka is in the garden also. Have you any news?"

"Rather!" replied the visitor, slowly screwing up his eyes, and protruding his lips. "Hm! here is a piece of news, if you please, and a very startling one, too. Fedor Ivanovich Lavretsky has arrived."

Ivan S. Turgenev

"Fedia!" exclaimed Marfa Timofeevna. "You're inventing, are you not?"

"Not at all. I have seen him with my own eyes."

"That doesn't prove any thing."

"He's grown much more robust," continued Gedeonovsky, looking as if he had not heard Marfa Timofeevna's remark; "his shoulders have broadened, and his cheeks are quite rosy."

"Grown more robust," slowly repeated Maria Dmitrievna. "One would think he hadn't met with much to make him robust."

"That is true indeed," said Gedeonovsky. "Any one else, in his place, would have scrupled to show himself in the world."

"And why, I should like to know?" broke in Marfa Timofeevna. "What nonsense you are talking! A man comes back to his home. Where else would you have him betake himself? And, pray, in what has he been to blame?"

"A husband is always to blame, madam, if you will allow me to say so, when his wife behaves ill."

"You only say that, *batyushka*,[A] because you have never been married."

[Footnote A: Father.]

Gedeonovsky's only reply was a forced smile. For a short time he remained silent, but presently he said, "May I be allowed to be so inquisitive as to ask for whom this pretty scarf is intended?"

Marfa Timofeevna looked up at him quickly.

"For whom is it intended?" she said. "For a man who never slanders, who does not intrigue, and who makes up no falsehoods—if, indeed, such a man is to be found in the world. I know Fedia thoroughly well; the only thing for which he is to blame is that he spoilt his wife. To be sure he married for love; and from such love-matches no good ever comes," added the old lady, casting a side glance at Maria Dmitrievna. Then, standing up, she added: "But now you can whet your teeth on whom you will; on me, if you like. I'm off. I won't hinder you any longer." And with these words she disappeared.

"She is always like that," said Maria Dmitrievna following her aunt with her eyes—"always."

"What else can be expected of her at her time of life?" replied Gedeonovsky. "Just see now! 'Who does not intrigue?' she was pleased to say. But who is there nowadays who doesn't intrigue? It is the custom of the present age. A friend of mine—a most respectable man, and one, I may as well observe, of no slight rank—used to say, 'Nowadays, it seems, if a hen wants a grain of corn she approaches it cunningly, watches anxiously for an opportunity of sidling up to it.' But when I look at you, dear lady, I recognize in you a truly angelic nature. May I be allowed to kiss your snow-white hand?"

Maria Dmitrievna slightly smiled, and held out her plump hand to Gedeonovsky, keeping the little finger gracefully separated from the rest; and then, after he had raised her hand to his lips, she drew her chair closer to his, bent a little towards him, and asked, in a low voice—

Ivan S. Turgenev

"So you have seen him? And is he really well and in good spirits?"

"In excellent spirits," replied Gedeonovsky in a whisper.

"You haven't heard where his wife is now?"

"A short time ago she was in Paris; but she is gone away, they say, and is now in Italy."

"Really it is shocking—Fedia's position. I can't think how he manages to bear it. Every one, of course, has his misfortunes; but his affairs, one may say, have become known all over Europe."

Gedeonovsky sighed.

"Quite so, quite so! They say she has made friends with artists and pianists; or, as they call them there, with lions and other wild beasts. She has completely lost all sense of shame—"

"It's very, very sad," said Maria Dmitrievna; "especially for a relation. You know, don't you, Sergius Petrovich, that he is a far-away cousin of mine?"

"To be sure, to be sure! You surely don't suppose I could be ignorant of any thing that concerns your family."

"Will he come to see us? What do you think?"

"One would suppose so; but afterwards, I am told, he will go and live on his estate in the country."

Maria Dmitrievna lifted her eyes towards heaven.

"Oh, Sergius Petrovich, Sergius Petrovich! how often I think how necessary it is for us women to behave circumspectly!"

"There are women and women, Maria Dmitrievna. There are, unfortunately, some who are—of an unstable character; and then there is a certain time of life—and, besides, good principles have not been instilled into them when they were young."

Here Sergius Petrovich drew from his pocket a blue handkerchief, of a check pattern, and began to unfold it.

"Such women, in fact, do exist."

Here Sergius Petrovich applied a corner of the handkerchief to each of his eyes in turn.

"But, generally speaking, if one reflects—that is to say—The dust in the streets is something extraordinary," he ended by saying.

"*Maman, maman,*" exclaimed a pretty little girl of eleven, who came running into the room, "Vladimir Nikolaevich is coming here on horseback."

Maria Dmitrievna rose from her chair. Sergius Petrovich also got up and bowed.

"My respects to Elena Mikhailovna," he said; and, discreetly retiring to a corner, he betook himself to blowing his long straight nose.

"What a lovely horse he has!" continued the little girl. "He was at the garden gate just now, and he told me and Liza that he would come up to the front door."

Ivan S. Turgenev

The sound of hoofs was heard, and a well appointed cavalier, mounted on a handsome bay horse, rode up to the house, and stopped in front of the open window.

III

"Good-evening, Maria Dmitrievna!" exclaimed the rider's clear and pleasant voice. "How do you like my new purchase?"

Maria Dmitrievna went to the window.

"Good-evening, Woldemar! Ah, what a splendid horse! From whom did you buy it?"

"From our remount-officer. He made me pay dear for it, the rascal."

"What is it's name?"

"Orlando. But that's a stupid name. I want to change it. *Eh bien, eh bien, mon garcon.* What a restless creature it is!"

The horse neighed, pawed the air, and tossed the foam from its nostrils.

"Come and stroke it, Lenochka; don't be afraid."

Lenochka stretched out her hand from the window, but Orlando suddenly reared and shied. But its rider, who took its proceedings very quietly, gripped the saddle firmly with his knees, laid his whip across the horse's neck, and forced it, in spite of its resistance, to return to the window, "*Prenez garde, prenez garde*," Maria Dmitrievna kept calling out.

"Now then, stroke him, Lenochka," repeated the horseman; "I don't mean to let him have his own way."

Lenochka stretched out her hand a second time, and timidly touched the quivering nostrils of Orlando, who champed his bit, and kept incessantly fidgeting.

"Bravo!" exclaimed Maria Dmitrievna; "but now get off, and come in."

The rider wheeled his horse sharply round, drove the spurs into its sides, rode down the street at a hand gallop, and turned into the court-yard. In another minute he had crossed the hall and entered the drawing-room, flourishing his whip in the air.

At the same moment there appeared on the threshold of another doorway a tall, well-made, dark-haired girl of nineteen—Maria Dmitrievna's elder daughter, Liza.

IV

The young man whom we have just introduced to our readers was called Vladimir Nikolaevich Panshine. He occupied a post at St. Petersburg—one devoted to business of a special character—in the Ministry of the Interior. He had come to O. about certain affairs of a temporary nature, and was placed there at the disposal of the governor, General Zonnenberg, to whom he was distantly related.

Panshine's father, a retired cavalry officer,[A] who used to be well known among card-players, was a man of a worn face, with weak eyes, and a nervous contraction about the lips. Throughout his life he always revolved in a distinguished circle, frequenting the English Clubs[B] of both capitals, and being generally considered a man of ability and a pleasant companion, though not a person to be confidently depended upon. In spite of all his ability, he was almost always just on the verge of ruin, and he ultimately left but a small and embarrassed property to his only son. About that son's education, however, he had, after his own fashion, taken great pains.

[Footnote A: A *Shtabs-Rotmistr*, the second captain in a cavalry regiment.]

[Footnote B: Fashionable clubs having nothing English about

them but their name.]

The young Vladimir Nikolaevich spoke excellent French, good English, and bad German. That is just as it should be. Properly brought-up people should of course be ashamed to speak German really well; but to throw out a German word now and then, and generally on facetious topics—that is allowable; "*c'est meme tres chic*," as the Petersburg Parisians say. Moreover, by the time Vladimir Nikolaevich was fifteen, he already knew how to enter any drawing-room whatsoever without becoming nervous, how to move about it in an agreeable manner, and how to take his leave exactly at the right moment.

The elder Panshine made a number of useful connections for his son; while shuffling the cards between two rubbers, or after a lucky "Great Schlemm,"[A] he never lost the opportunity of saying a word about his young "Volodka" to some important personage, a lover of games of skill. On his part, Vladimir Nikolaevich, during the period of his stay at the university, which he left with the rank of "effective student,"[B] made acquaintance with several young people of distinction, and gained access into the best houses. He was cordially received everywhere, for he was very good looking, easy in manner, amusing, always in good health, and ready for every thing. Where he was obliged, he was respectful; where he could, he was overbearing. Altogether, an excellent companion, *un charmant garcon*. The Promised Land lay before him. Panshine soon fathomed the secret of worldly wisdom, and succeeded in inspiring himself with a genuine respect for its laws. He knew how to invest trifles with a half-ironical importance, and to behave with the air of one who treats all serious matters as trifles. He danced admirably; he dressed like an Englishman. In a short time he had gained the reputation of being one of the pleasantest and most adroit young men in St. Petersburg.

[Footnote A: "A bumper."]

[Footnote B: A degree a little inferior to that of Bachelor of Arts.]

Panshine really was very adroit—not less so than his father had been. And besides this, he was endowed with no small talent; nothing was too difficult for him. He sang pleasantly, drew confidently, could write poetry, and acted remarkably well.

He was now only in his twenty eighth year, but he was already a Chamberlain, and he had arrived at a highly respectable rank in the service. He had thorough confidence in himself, in his intellect, and in his sagacity. He went onwards under full sail, boldly and cheerfully; the stream of his life flowed smoothly along. He was accustomed to please every one, old and young alike; and he imagined that he thoroughly understood his fellow-creatures, especially women—that he was intimately acquainted with all their ordinary weaknesses.

As one who was no stranger to Art, he felt within him a certain enthusiasm, a glow, a rapture, in consequence of which he claimed for himself various exemptions from ordinary rules. He led a somewhat irregular life, he made acquaintance with people who were not received into society, and in general he behaved in an unconventional and unceremonious manner. But in his heart of hearts he was cold and astute; and even in the midst of his most extravagant rioting, his keen hazel eye watched and took note of every thing. It was impossible for this daring and unconventional youth ever quite to forget himself, or to be thoroughly carried away. It should be mentioned to his credit, by the way, that he never boasted of his victories. To Maria Dmitrievna's house he had obtained access as soon as he arrived in O., and he soon made himself thoroughly at home in it. As to Maria Dmitrievna herself, she thought there was nobody in the world to be compared with him.

Panshine bowed in an engaging manner to all the occupants of the room; shook hands with Maria Dmitrievna and Elizaveta Mikhailovna, lightly tapped Gedeonovsky on the shoulder, and, turning on his heels, took Lenochka's head between his hands and kissed her on the forehead.

"Are not you afraid to ride such a vicious horse?" asked Maria Dmitrievna.

"I beg your pardon, it is perfectly quiet. No, but I will tell you what I really am afraid of. I am afraid of playing at preference with Sergius Petrovich. Yesterday, at the Bielenitsines', he won all the money I had with me."

Gedeonovsky laughed a thin and cringing laugh; he wanted to gain the good graces of the brilliant young official from St. Petersburg, the governor's favorite. In his conversations with Maria Dmitrievna, he frequently spoke of Panshine's remarkable faculties. "Why, really now, how can one help praising him?" he used to reason. "The young man is a success in the highest circles of society, and at the same time he does his work in the most perfect manner, and he isn't the least bit proud." And indeed, even at St. Petersburg, Panshine was looked upon as an efficient public servant; the work "burnt under his hands;" he spoke of it jestingly, as a man of the world should, who does not attach any special importance to his employment; but he was a "doer." Heads of departments like such subordinates; he himself never doubted that in time, supposing he really wished it, he would be a Minister.

"You are so good as to say that I won your money," said

Gedeonovsky; "but who won fifteen roubles from me last week? And besides—"

"Ah, rogue, rogue!" interrupted Panshine, in a pleasant tone, but with an air of indifference bordering on contempt, and then, without paying him any further attention, he accosted Liza.

"I cannot get the overture to Oberon here," he began. "Madame Bielenitsine boasted that she had a complete collection of classical music; but in reality she has nothing but polkas and waltzes. However, I have already written to Moscow, and you shall have the overture in a week."

"By the way," he continued, "I wrote a new romance yesterday; the words are mine as well as the music. Would you like me to sing it to you? Madame Bielenitsine thought it very pretty, but her judgment is not worth much. I want to know your opinion of it. But, after all, I think I had better sing it by-and-by."

"Why by-and-by?" exclaimed Maria Dmitrievna, "why not now?"

"To hear is to obey," answered Panshine, with a sweet and serene smile, which came and went quickly; and then, having pushed a chair up to the piano, he sat down, struck a few chords, and began to sing the following romance, pronouncing the words very distinctly

Amid pale clouds, above the earth,
The moon rides high,
And o'er the sea a magic light
Pours from the sky.

My Spirit's waves, as towards the moon,

Towards thee, love, flow:
Its waters stirred by thee alone
In weal or woe.

My heart replete with love that grieves
But yields no cry,
I suffer—cold as yonder moon
Thou passest by.

Panshine sang the second stanza with more than usual expression and feeling; in the stormy accompaniment might be heard the rolling of the waves. After the words, "I suffer!" he breathed a light sigh, and with downcast eyes let his voice die gradually away. When he had finished; Liza praised the air, Maria Dmitrievna said, "Charming!" and Gedeonovsky exclaimed, "Enchanting!—the words and the music are equally enchanting!" Lenochka kept her eyes fixed on the singer with childish reverence. In a word, the composition of the young *dilettante* delighted all who were in the room. But outside the drawing-room door, in the vestibule, there stood, looking on the floor, an old man who had just come into the house, to whom, judging from the expression of his face and the movements of his shoulders, Panshine's romance, though really pretty, did not afford much pleasure. After waiting a little, and having dusted his boots with a coarse hand-kerchief, he suddenly squeezed up his eyes, morosely compressed his lips, gave his already curved back an extra bend, and slowly entered the drawing-room.

"Ah! Christophor Fedorovich, how do you do?" Panshine was the first to exclaim, as he jumped up quickly from his chair. "I didn't suspect you were there. I wouldn't for any thing have ventured to sing my romance before you. I know you are no admirer of the light style in music."

"I didn't hear it," said the new-comer, in imperfect Russian.

Then, having bowed to all the party, he stood still in an awkward attitude in the middle of the room.

"I suppose, Monsieur Lemm," said Maria Dmitrievna, "you have come to give Liza a music lesson."

"No; not Lizaveta Mikhailovna, but Elena Miknailovna."

"Oh, indeed! very good. Lenochka, go up-stairs with Monsieur Lemm."

The old man was about to follow the little girl, when Panshine stopped him.

"Don't go away when the lesson is over, Christopher Fedorovich," he said. "Lizaveta Mikhailovna and I are going to play a duet—one of Beethoven's sonatas."

The old man muttered something to himself, but Panshine continued in German, pronouncing the words very badly—

"Lizaveta Mikhailovna has shown me the sacred cantata which you have dedicated to her—a very beautiful piece! I beg you will not suppose I am unable to appreciate serious music. Quite the reverse. It is sometimes tedious; but, on the other hand, it is extremely edifying."

The old man blushed to the ears, cast a side glance at Liza, and went hastily out of the room.

Maria Dmitrievna asked Panshine to repeat his romance; but he declared that he did not like to offend the ears of the scientific German, and proposed to Liza to begin Beethoven's sonata. On this, Maria Dmitrievna sighed, and, on her part, proposed a stroll in the garden to Gedeonovsky.

"I want to have a little more chat with you," she said, "about our poor Fedia, and to ask for your advice."

Gedeonovsky smiled and bowed, took up with two fingers his hat, on the brim of which his gloves were neatly laid out, and retired with Maria Dmitrievna.

Panshine and Eliza remained in the room. She fetched the sonata, and spread it out. Both sat down to the piano in silence. From up-stairs there came the feeble sound of scales, played by Lenochka's uncertain fingers.

*   *   *   *   *

Note to p. 36.

It is possible that M. Panshine may have been inspired by Heine's verses:—

Wie des Mondes Abbild zittert
In den wilden Meereswogen,
Und er selber still und sicher
Wandelt an dem Himmelshogen.

Also wandelst du, Geliebte,
Still und sicher, und es zittert
Nur dein Abbild mir im Herzen,
Weil mein eignes Herz erschuettert.

V

Christoph Theodor Gottlieb Lemm was born in 1786, in the kingdom of Saxony, in the town of Chemnitz. His parents, who were very poor, were both of them musicians, his father playing the hautboy, his mother the harp. He himself, by the time he was five years old, was already practicing on three different instruments. At the age of eight, he was left an orphan, and at ten, he began to earn a living by his art. For a long time he led a wandering life, playing in all sorts of places—in taverns, at fairs, at peasants' marriages, and at balls. At last he gained access to an orchestra, and there, steadily rising higher and higher, he attained to the position of conductor. As a performer he had no great merit, but he understood music thoroughly. In his twenty-eighth year, he migrated to Russia. He was invited there by a great seigneur, who, although he could not abide music himself, maintained an orchestra from a love of display. In his house Lemm spent seven years as a musical director, and then left him with empty hands. The seigneur, who had squandered all his means, first offered Lemm a bill of exchange for the amount due to him; then refused to give him even that; and ultimately never paid him a single farthing. Lemm was advised to leave the country, but he did not like to go home penniless from Russia—from the great Russia, that golden land of artists. So be determined to remain and seek his fortune there.

During the course of ten years, the poor German continued to seek his fortune. He found various employers, he lived in Moscow, and in several county towns, he patiently suffered much, he made acquaintance with poverty, he struggled hard.[A] All this time, amidst all the troubles to which he was exposed, the idea of ultimately returning home never quitted him. It was the only thing that supported him. But fate did not choose to bless him with this supreme and final piece of good fortune.

[Footnote A: Literally, "like a fish out of ice:" as a fish, taken out of a river which has been frozen over, struggles on the ice.]

At fifty years of age, in bad health and prematurely decrepid, he happened to come to the town of O., and there he took up his permanent abode, managing somehow to obtain a poor livelihood by giving lessons. He had by this time entirely lost all hope of quilting the hated soil of Russia.

Lemm's outward appearance was not in his favor. He was short and high-shouldered, his shoulder-blades stuck out awry, his feet were large and flat, and his red hands, marked by swollen veins, had hard, stiff fingers, tipped with nails of a pale blue color. His face was covered with wrinkles, his cheeks were hollow, and he had pursed-up lips which he was always moving with a kind of chewing action—one which, joined with his habitual silence, gave him an almost malignant expression. His grey hair hung in tufts over a low forehead. His very small and immobile eyes glowed dully, like coals in which the flame has just been extinguished by water. He walked heavily, jerking his clumsy frame at every step. Some of his movements called to mind the awkward shuffling of an owl in a cage, when it feels that it is being stared at, but can scarcely see anything itself out of its large yellow eyes, blinking between sleep and fear. An ancient and inexorable misery had fixed its ineffaceable stamp on the poor musician, and had wrenched and distorted his figure—one which, even without that, would have had but little to recommend it; but in spite of all that, something good and honest, something out of the common run, revealed itself in that half-ruined being, to any one who was able to get over his first impressions.

A devoted admirer of Bach and Handel, thoroughly well up to his work, gifted with a lively imagination, and that audacity of idea which belongs only to the Teutonic race, Lemm might in time—who can tell?—have been reckoned among the great composers of his country, if only his life had been of a different nature. But he was not born under a lucky star. He had written much in his time, and yet he had never been fortunate enough to see any of his compositions published. He did not know how to set to work, how to cringe at the right moment, how to proffer a request at the fitting time. Once, it is true, a very long time ago, one of his friends and admirers, also a German, and also poor, published at his own expense two of Lemm's sonatas. But they remained untouched on the shelves of the music shops; silently they disappeared and left no trace behind, just as if they had been dropped into a river by night.

At last Lemm bade farewell to every thing Old age gained upon him, and he hardened, he grew stiff in mind, just as his fingers had stiffened. He had never married, and now he lived alone in O., in a little house not far from that of the Kalitines, looked after by an old woman-servant whom he had taken out of an alms-house. He walked a great deal, and he read the Bible, also a collection of Protestant hymns, and Shakspeare in Schlegel's translation. For a long time he had composed nothing; but apparently Liza, his best pupil, had been able to arouse him. It was for her that he had written the cantata to which Panshine alluded. The words of this cantata were borrowed by him from his collection of hymns, with the exception of a few verses which he composed himself. It was written for two choruses: one of the happy, one of the unhappy. At the end the two united and sang together, "Merciful Lord, have pity upon us, poof sinners, and keep us from all evil thoughts and worldly desires." On the title-page, very carefully and even artistically written, were the words, "Only the Righteous are in the Right. A Sacred Cantata. Composed, and dedicated to Elizaveta Kalitine, his dear pupil, by her teacher, C.T.G, Lemm." The words "Only the Righteous are in the Right." and "To Elizaveta Kalitine" were surrounded by a circle of rays. Underneath was written, "For you only. Fuer Sie allein." This was why Lemm grew red and looked askance at Liza; he felt greatly hurt when Panshine began to talk to him about his cantata.

VI

Panshine struck the first chords of the sonata, in which he played the bass, loudly and with decision, but Liza did not begin her part. He stopped and looked at her—Liza's eyes, which were looking straight at him, expressed dissatisfaction; her lips did not smile, all her countenance was severe, almost sad.

"What is the matter?" he asked.

"Why have you not kept your word?" she said. "I showed you Christopher Fedorovich's cantata only on condition that you would not speak to him about it."

"I was wrong, Lizaveta Mikhailovna—I spoke without thinking."

"You have wounded him and me too. In future he will distrust me as well as others."

"What could I do, Lizaveta Mikhailovna? From my earliest youth I have never been able to see a German without feeling tempted to tease him."

"What are you saying, Vladimir Nikolaevich? This German is a poor, lonely, broken man; and you feel no pity for him!

Ivan S. Turgenev

you feel tempted to tease him!"

Panshine seemed a little disconcerted.

"You are right, Lizaveta Mikhailovna," he said "The fault is entirely due to my perpetual thoughtlessness. No, do not contradict me. I know myself well. My thoughtlessness has done me no slight harm. It makes people suppose that I am an egotist."

Panshine made a brief pause. From whatever point he started a conversation, he generally ended by speaking about himself, and then his words seemed almost to escape from him involuntarily, so softly and pleasantly did he speak, and with such an air of sincerity.

"It is so, even in your house," he continued. "Your mamma, it is true, is most kind to me. She is so good. You—but no, I don't know what you think of me. But decidedly your aunt cannot abide me. I have vexed her by some thoughtless, stupid speech. It is true that she does not like me, is it not?"

"Yes," replied Liza, after a moment's hesitation. "You do not please her."

Panshine let his fingers run rapidly over the keys; a scarcely perceptible smile glided over his lips.

"Well, but you," he continued, "do you also think me an egotist?".

"I know so little about you," replied Liza; "but I should not call you an egotist. On the contrary, I ought to feel grateful to you—"

"I know, I know what you are going to say," interrupted

Panshine, again running his fingers over the keys, "for the music, for the books, which I bring you, for the bad drawings with which I ornament your album, and so on, and so on. I may do all that, and yet be an egotist. I venture to think that I do not bore you, and that you do not think me a bad man; but yet you suppose that I—how shall I say it?—for the sake of an epigram would not spare my friend, my father him self."

"You are absent and forgetful, like all men of the world," said Liza, "that is all."

Panshine slightly frowned.

"Listen," he said; "don't let's talk any more about me; let us begin our sonata. Only there is one thing I will ask of you," he added, as he smoothed the sheets which lay on the music-desk with his hand; "think of me what you will, call me egotist even, I don't object to that; but don't call me a man of the world, that name is insufferable. *Anch'io sono pittore.* I too am an artist, though but a poor one, and that—namely, that I am a poor artist—I am going to prove to you on the spot. Let us begin."

"Very good, let us begin," said Liza.

The first adagio went off with tolerable success, although Panshine made several mistakes. What he had written himself, and what he had learnt by heart, he played very well, but he could not play at sight correctly. Accordingly the second part of the sonata—tolerably quick allegro—would not do at all. At the twentieth bar Panshine, who was a couple of bars behind, gave in, and pushed back his chair with a laugh.

"No!" he exclaimed, "I cannot play to-day. It is fortunate that Lemm cannot hear us; he would have had a fit."

　　　　　Ivan S. Turgenev

Liza stood up, shut the piano, and then turned to Panshine.

"What shall we do then?" she asked.

"That question is so like you! You can never sit with folded hands for a moment. Well then, if you feel inclined, let's draw a little before it becomes quite dark. Perhaps another Muse—the Muse of painting—what's her name? I've forgotten—will be more propitious to me. Where is your album? I remember the landscape I was drawing in it was not finished."

Liza went into another room for the album, and Panshine, finding himself alone, took a cambric handkerchief out of his pocket, rubbed his nails and looked sideways at his hands. They were very white and well shaped; on the second finger of the left hand he wore a spiral gold ring.

Liza returned; Panshine seated himself by the window and opened the album.

"Ah!" he exclaimed, "I see you have begun to copy my landscape—and capitally—very good indeed—only—just give me the pencil—the shadows are not laid in black enough. Look here."

And Panshine added some long strokes with a vigorous touch. He always drew the same landscape—large dishevelled trees in the foreground, in the middle distance a plain, and on the horizon an indented chain of hills. Liza looked over his shoulder at his work.

"In drawing, as also in life in general," said Panshine, turning his head now to the right, now to the left, "lightness and daring—those are the first requisites."

At this moment Lemm entered the room, and after bowing gravely, was about to retire; but Panshine flung the album and pencil aside, and prevented him from leaving the room.

"Where are you going, dear Christoph Fedorovich? Won't you stay and take tea?"

"I am going home," said Lemm, in a surly voice; "my head aches."

"What nonsense! do remain. We will have a talk about Shakspeare."

"My head aches," repeated the old man.

"We tried to play Beethoven's sonata without you," continued Panshine, caressingly throwing his arm over the old man's shoulder and smiling sweetly; "but we didn't succeed in bringing it to a harmonious conclusion. Just imagine, I couldn't play two consecutive notes right."

"You had better have played your romance over again," replied Lemm; then, escaping from Panshine's hold he went out of the room.

Liza ran after him, and caught him on the steps.

"Christopher Fedorovich, I want to speak to you," she said in German, as led him across the short green grass to the gate. "I have done you a wrong—forgive me."

Lemm made no reply.

"I showed your cantata to Vladimir Nikolaevich; I was sure he would appreciate it, and, indeed, he was exceedingly pleased with it."

Lemm stopped still.

"It's no matter," he said in Russian, and then added in his native tongue,—"But he is utterly incapable of understanding it. How is it you don't see that? He is a *dilettante*—that is all."

"You are unjust towards him," replied Liza. "He understands every thing, and can do almost every thing himself."

"Yes, every thing second-rate—poor goods, scamped work. But that pleases, and he pleases, and he is well content with that. Well, then, bravo!—But I am not angry. I and that cantata, we are both old fools! I feel a little ashamed, but it's no matter."

"Forgive me, Christopher Fedorovich!" urged Liza anew.

"It's no matter, no matter," he repeated a second time in Russian. "You are a good girl.—Here is some one coming to pay you a visit. Good-bye. You are a very good girl."

And Lemm made his way with hasty steps to the gate, through which there was passing a gentleman who was a stranger to him, dressed in a grey paletot and a broad straw hat. Politely saluting him (he bowed to every new face in O., and always turned away his head from his acquaintances in the street—such was the rule he had adopted), Lemm went past him, and disappeared behind the wall.

The stranger gazed at him as he retired with surprise, then looked at Liza, and then went straight up to her.

VII

"You won't remember me," he said, as he took off his hat, "but I recognized you, though it is seven years since I saw you last. You were a child then. I am Lavretsky. Is your mamma at home? Can I see her?"

"Mamma will be so glad," replied Liza. "She has heard of your arrival."

"Your name is Elizaveta, isn't it?" asked Lavretsky, as he mounted the steps leading up to the house.

"Yes."

"I remember you perfectly. Yours was even in those days one of the faces which one does not forget. I used to bring you sweetmeats then."

Liza blushed a little, and thought to herself, "What an odd man!" Lavretsky stopped for a minute in the hall.

Liza entered the drawing-room, in which Panshine's voice and laugh were making themselves heard. He was communicating some piece of town gossip to Maria Dmitrievna and Gedeonovsky, both of whom had by this time returned from the garden, and he was laughly loudly at his own story. At the name of Lavretsky, Maria Dmitrievna became nervous and turned pale, but went forward to receive him.

"How are you? how are you, my dear cousin?" she exclaimed, with an almost lachrymose voice, dwelling on each word she uttered. "How glad I am to see you!"

"How are you, my good cousin?" replied Lavretsky, with a friendly pressure of her outstretched hand. "Is all well with you?"

"Sit clown, sit down, my dear Fedor Ivanovich. Oh, how delighted I am! But first let me introduce my daughter Liza."

"I have already introduced myself to Lizaveta Mikhailovna," interrupted Lavretsky.

"Monsieur Panshine—Sergius Petrovich Gedeonovsky. But do sit down. I look at you, and, really, I can scarcely trust my eyes. But tell me about your health; is it good?"

"I am quite well, as you can see. And you, too, cousin—if I can say so without bringing you bad luck[A]—you are none the worse for these seven years."

[Footnote A: A reference to the superstition of the "evil eye," still rife among the peasants in Russia. Though it has died out among the educated classes, yet the phrase, "not to cast an evil eye," is still made use of in conversation.]

"When I think what a number of years it is since we last saw one another," musingly said Maria Dmitrievna. "Where do you come from now? Where have you left—that's to say, I meant"—she hurriedly corrected herself—"I meant to say, shall you stay with us long?"

"I come just now from Berlin," replied Lavretsky, "and to-morrow I shall go into the country—to stay there, in all probability, a long time."

"I suppose you are going to live at Lavriki?"

"No, not at Lavriki; but I have a small property about five-and-twenty versts from here, and I am going there."

"Is that the property which Glafira Petrovna left you?"

"Yes, that's it."

"But really, Fedor Ivanovich, you have such a charming house at Lavriki."

Lavretsky frowned a little.

"Yes—but I have a cottage on the other estate too; I don't require any more just now. That place is—most convenient for me at present."

Maria Dmitrievna became once more so embarrassed that she actually sat upright in her chair, and let her hands drop by her side. Panshine came to the rescue, and entered into conversation with Lavretsky. Maria Dmitrievna by degrees grew calm, leant back again comfortably in her chair, and from time to time contributed a word or two to the conversation. But still she kept looking at her guest so pitifully, sighing so significantly, and shaking her head so sadly, that at last he lost all patience, and asked her, somewhat brusquely, if she was unwell.

"No, thank God!" answered Maria Dmitrievna; "but why do you ask?"

"Because I thought you did not seem quite yourself."

Maria Dmitrievna assumed a dignified and somewhat offended expression.

"If that's the way you take it," she thought, "it's a matter of perfect indifference to me; it's clear that every thing slides off you like water off a goose. Any one else would have withered up with misery, but you've grown fat on it."

Maria Dmitrievna did not stand upon ceremony when she was only thinking to herself. When she spoke aloud she was more choice in her expressions.

And in reality Lavretsky did not look like a victim of destiny. His rosy-cheeked, thoroughly Russian face, with its large white forehead, somewhat thick nose, and long straight lips, seemed to speak of robust health and enduring vigor of constitution. He was powerfully built, and his light hair twined in curls, like a boy's, about his head. Only in his eyes, which were blue, rather prominent, and a little wanting in mobility, an expression might be remarked which it would be difficult to define. It might have been melancholy, or it might have been fatigue; and the ring of his voice seemed somewhat monotonous.

All this time Panshine was supporting the burden of the conversation. He brought it round to the advantages of sugar making, about which he had lately read two French pamphlets; their contents he now proceeded to disclose, speaking with an air of great modesty, but without saying a single word about the sources of his information.

"Why, there's Fedia!" suddenly exclaimed the voice of Marfa Timofeevna in the next room, the door of which had been left half open. "Actually, Fedia!" And the old lady hastily entered the room. Lavretsky hadn't had time to rise from his chair before she had caught him in her arms. "Let me have a look at you," she exclaimed, holding him at a little distance from her. "Oh, how well you are looking! You've grown a little older, but you haven't altered a bit for the worse, that's a fact. But what makes you kiss my hand. Kiss my face, if you please, unless you don't like the look of my wrinkled cheeks. I dare say you never asked after me, or whether your aunt was alive or no. And yet it was my hands received you when you first saw the light, you good-for-nothing fellow! Ah, well, it's all one. But it was a good idea of yours to come here. I say, my dear," she suddenly exclaimed, turning to Maria Dmitrievna, "have you offered him any refreshment?"

"I don't want any thing," hastily said Lavretsky.

"Well, at all events, you will drink tea with us, *batyushka*. Gracious heavens! A man comes, goodness knows from how far off, and no one gives him so much as a cup of tea. Liza, go and see after it quickly. I remember he was a terrible glutton when he was a boy, and even now, perhaps, he is fond of eating and drinking."

"Allow me to pay my respects, Maria Timofeevna," said Panshine, coming up to the excited old lady, and making her a low bow.

"Pray excuse me, my dear sir," replied Marfa Timofeevna, "I overlooked you in my joy. You're just like your dear mother," she continued, turning anew to Lavretsky, "only you always had your father's nose, and you have it still. Well, shall you stay here long?"

"I go away to-morrow, aunt."

"To where?".

"To my house at Vasilievskoe."

"To-morrow?"

"To-morrow."

"Well, if it must be to-morrow, so be it. God be with you! You know what is best for yourself. Only mind you come and say good-bye." The old lady tapped him gently on the cheek. "I didn't suppose I should live to see you come back; not that I thought I was going to die—no, no; I have life enough left in me for ten years to come. All we Pestofs are long-lived—your late grandfather used to call us double-lived; but God alone could tell how long you were going to loiter abroad. Well, well! You are a fine fellow—a very fine fellow. I dare say you can still lift ten poods[A] with one hand, as you used to do. Your late father, if you'll excuse my saying so, was as nonsensical as he could be, but he did well in getting you that Swiss tutor. Do you remember the boxing matches you used to have with him? Gymnastics, wasn't it, you used to call them? But why should I go on cackling like this? I shall only prevent Monsieur Pan*shine* (she never laid the accent on the first syllable of his name, as she ought to have done) from favoring us with his opinions. On the whole, we had much better go and have tea. Yes, let's go and have it on the terrace. We have magnificent cream—not like what they have in your Londons and Parises. Come away, come away; and you, Fediouchka, give me your arm. What a strong arm you have, to be sure! I shan't fall while you're by my side."

[Footnote A: The pood weighs thirty-six pounds.]

Every one rose and went out on the terrace, except Gedeonovsky, who slipped away stealthily. During the whole time Lavretsky was talking with the mistress of the house, with Panshine and with Marfa Timofeevna, that old gentleman had been sitting in his corner, squeezing up his eyes and shooting out his lips, while he listened with the curiosity of a child to all that was being said. When he left, it was that he might hasten to spread through the town the news of the recent arrival.

Here is a picture of what was taking place at eleven o'clock that same evening in the Kalitines' house. Down stairs, on the threshold of the drawing-room, Panshine was taking leave of Liza, and saying, as he held her hand in his:—

"You know who it is that attracts me here; you know why I am always coming to your house. Of what use are words when all is so clear?"

Liza did not say a word in reply—she did not ever smile. Slightly arching her eyebrows, and growing rather red, she kept her eyes fixed on the ground, but did not withdraw her hand. Up stairs, in Marfa Timofeevna's room, the light of the lamp, which hung in the corner before the age-embrowned sacred pictures, fell on Lavretsky, as he sat in an arm-chair, his elbows resting on his knees, his face hidden in his hands. In front of him stood the old lady, who from time to time silently passed her hand over his hair. He spent more than an hour with her after taking leave of the mistress of the house, he scarcely saying a word to his kind old friend, and she not asking him any questions. And why should he have spoken? what could she have asked? She understood all so well, she so fully sympathized with all the feelings which filled his heart.

Ivan S. Turgenev

VIII

Fedor Ivanovich Lavretsky (we must ask our reader's permission to break off the thread of the story for a time) sprang from a noble family of long descent. The founder of the race migrated from Prussia during the reign of Basil the Blind,[A] and was favored with a grant of two hundred *chetverts*[B] of land in the district of Biejetsk. Many of his descendants filled various official positions, and were appointed to governorships in distant places, under princes and influential personages, but none of them obtained any great amount of property, or arrived at a higher dignity, than that of inspector of the Czar's table.

[Footnote A: In the fifteenth century.]

[Footnote B: An old measure of land, variously estimated at from two to six acres.]

The richest and most influential of all the Lavretskys was Fedor Ivanovich's paternal great-grandfather Andrei, a man who was harsh, insolent, shrewd, and crafty. Even up to the present day men have never ceased to talk about his despotic manners, his furious temper, his senseless prodigality, and his insatiable avarice. He was very tall and stout, his complexion was swarthy, and he wore no beard. He lisped, and he generally seemed half asleep. But the more quietly he spoke, the more did all around him tremble. He had found a wife not unlike himself. She had a round face, a yellow complexion, prominent eyes, and the nose of a hawk. A gypsy by descent, passionate and vindictive in temper, she refused to yield in any thing to her husband, who all but brought her to her grave, and whom, although she had been eternally squabbling with him, she could net bear long to survive.

Andrei's son, Peter, our Fedor's grandfather, did not take after his father. He was a simple country gentleman; rather odd, noisy in voice and slow in action, rough but not malicious, hospitable, and devoted to coursing. He was more than thirty years old when he inherited from his father two thousand souls,[A] all in excellent condition; but he soon began to squander his property, a part of which he disposed of by sale, and he spoilt his household. His large, warm, and dirty rooms were full of people of small degree, known and unknown, who swarmed in from all sides like cockroaches. All these visitors gorged themselves with whatever came in their way, drank their fill to intoxication, and carried off what they could, extolling and glorifying their affable host. As for their host, when he was out of humor with them, he called them scamps and parasites; but when deprived of their company, he soon found himself bored.

[Footnote A: Male serfs.]

The wife of Peter Andreich was a quiet creature whom he had taken from a neighboring family in acquiescence with his father's choice and command. Her name was Anna Pavlovna. She never interfered in any thing, received her guests cordially, and went out into society herself with pleasure—although "it was death" to her, to use her own phrase, to have to powder herself. "They put a felt cap on your head," she used to say in her old age; "they combed all

Ivan S. Turgenev

your hair straight up on end, they smeared it with grease, they strewed it with flour, they stuck it full of iron pins; you couldn't wash it away afterwards. But to pay a visit without powdering was impossible. People would have taken offence. What a torment it was!" She liked to drive fast, and was ready to play at cards from morning until evening. When her husband approached the card-table, she was always in the habit of covering with her hand the trumpery losses scored up against her; but she had made over to him, without reserve, all her dowry, all the money she had. She brought him two children—a son named Ivan, our Fedor's father, and a daughter, Glafira.[A]

[Footnote A: The accent should be on the second syllable of this name.]

Ivan was not brought up at home, but in the house of an old and wealthy maiden aunt, Princess Kubensky. She styled him her heir (if it had not been for that, his father would not have let him go), dressed him like a doll, gave him teachers of every kind, and placed him under the care of a French tutor—an ex-abbe, a pupil of Jean Jacques Rousseau—a certain M. Courtin de Vaucelles an adroit and subtle intriguer—"the very *fine fleur* of the emigration," as she expressed herself; and she ended by marrying this *fine fleur* when she was almost seventy years old. She transferred all her property to his name, and soon afterwards, rouged, perfumed with amber *a la Richelieu*, surrounded by negro boys, Italian grey-hounds, and noisy parrots, she died, stretched on a crooked silken couch of the style of Louis the Fifteenth, with an enamelled snuff-box of Petitot's work in her hands—and died deserted by her husband. The insinuating M. Courtin had preferred to take himself and her money off to Paris.

Ivan was in his twentieth year when this unexpected blow

struck him. We speak of the Princess's marriage, not her death. In his aunt's house, in which he had suddenly passed from the position of a wealthy heir to that of a hanger-on, he would not slay any longer. In Petersburg, the society in which he had grown up closed its doors upon him. For the lower ranks of the public service, and the laborious and obscure life they involved, he felt a strong repugnance. All this, it must be remembered, took place in the earliest part of the reign of the Emperor Alexander I[A]. He was obliged, greatly against his will, to return to his father's country house. Dirty, poor, and miserable did the paternal nest seem to him. The solitude and the dullness of a retired country life offended him at every step. He was devoured by ennui; besides, every one in the house, except his mother, regarded him with unloving eyes. His father disliked his metropolitan habits, his dress-coats and shirt-frills, his books, his flute, his cleanliness—from which he justly argued that his son regarded him with a feeling of aversion. He was always grumbling at his son, and complaining of his conduct.

[Footnote A: When corruption was the rule in the public service.]

"Nothing we have here pleases him," he used to say. "He is so fastidious at table, he eats nothing. He cannot bear the air and the smell of the room. The sight of drunken people upsets him; and as to beating anyone before him, you musn't dare to do it. Then he won't enter the service; his health is delicate, forsooth! Bah! What an effeminate creature!—and all because his head is full of Voltaire!" The old man particularly disliked Voltaire, and also the "infidel" Diderot, although he had never read a word of their works. Reading was not in his line.

Peter Andreich was not mistaken. Both Diderot and Voltaire really were in his son's head; and not they alone. Rousseau

Ivan S. Turgenev

and Raynal and Helvetius also, and many other similar writers, were in his head; but in his head only. Ivan Petrovich's former tutor, the retired Abbe and encyclopaedist, had satisfied himself with pouring all the collective wisdom of the eighteenth century over his pupil; and so the pupil existed, saturated with it. It held its own in him without mixing with his blood, without sinking into his mind, without resolving into fixed convictions. And would it be reasonable to ask for convictions from a youngster half a century ago, when we have not even yet acquired any?

Ivan Petrovich disconcerted the visitors also in his father's house. He was too proud to have anything to do with them; they feared him. With his sister Glafira, too, who was twelve years his senior, he did not at all agree. This Glafira was a strange being. Plain, deformed, meagre—with staring and severe eyes, and with thin, compressed lips—she, in her face and her voice, and in her angular and quick movements, resembled her grandmother, the gipsy Andrei's wife. Obstinate, and fond of power, she would not even hear of marriage. Ivan Petrovich's return home was by no means to her taste. So long as the Princess Kubensky kept him with her, Glafira had hoped to obtain at least half of her father's property; and in her avarice, as well as in other points, she resembled her grandmother. Besides this, Glafira was jealous of her brother. He had been educated so well; he spoke French so correctly, with a Parisian accent; and she scarcely knew how to say *"Bonjour"* and *"Comment vous portez vous?"* It is true that her parents were entirely ignorant of French, but that did not make things any better for her.

As to Ivan Petrovich, he did not know what to do with himself for vexation and ennui; he had not spent quite a year in the country, but even this time seemed to him like ten years. It was only with his mother that he was at ease in spirit; and for whole hours he used to sit in her low suite of rooms listening to the good lady's simple, unconnected talk, and stuffing himself with preserves. It happened that among Anna Pavlovna's maids there was a very pretty girl named Malania. Intelligent and modest, with calm, sweet eyes, and finely-cut features, she pleased Ivan Petrovich from the very first, and he soon fell in love with her. He loved her timid gait, her modest replies, her gentle voice, her quiet smile. Every day she seemed to him more attractive than before. And she attached herself to Ivan Petrovich with the whole strength of her soul—as only Russian girls know how to devote themselves—and gave herself to him. In a country house no secret can be preserved long; in a short time almost every one knew of the young master's fondness for Malania. At last the news reached Peter Andreich himself. At another time it is probable that he would have paid very little attention to so unimportant an affair; but he had long nursed a grudge against his son, and he was delighted to have an opportunity of disgracing the philosophical exquisite from St. Petersburg. There ensued a storm, attended by noise and outcry. Malania was locked up in the store-room.[A] Ivan Petrovich was summoned into his father's presence. Anna Pavlovna also came running to the scene of confusion, and tried to appease her husband; but he would not listen to a word she said. Like a hawk, he pounced upon his son charging him with immorality, atheism, and hypocrisy. He eagerly availed himself of so good an opportunity of discharging on him all his long-gathered spite against the Princess Kubensky, and overwhelmed him with insulting expressions.

[Footnote A: A sort of closet under the stairs.]

At first Ivan Petrovich kept silence, and maintained his hold over himself; but when his father thought fit to threaten him with a disgraceful punishment, he could bear it no longer. "Ah!" he thought, "the infidel Diderot is going to be brought

Ivan S. Turgenev

forward again. Well, then, I will put his teaching in action." And so with a quiet and even voice, although with a secret shuddering in all his limbs, he told his father that it was a mistake to accuse him of immorality; that he had no intention of justifying his fault, but that he was ready to make amends for it, and that all the more willingly, inasmuch as he felt himself superior to all prejudices; and, in fact—that he was ready to marry Malania. In uttering these words Ivan Petrovich undoubtedly attained the end he had in view. Peter Andreich was so confounded that he opened his eyes wide, and for a moment was struck dumb; but he immediately recovered his senses, and then and there, just as he was, wrapped in a dressing-gown trimmed with squirrels' fur, and with slippers on his bare feet, he rushed with clenched fists at his son, who, as if on purpose, had dressed his hair that day *a la Titus*, and had put on a blue dress-coat, quite new and made in the English fashion, tasselled boots, and dandified, tight-fitting buckskin pantaloons. Anna Pavlovna uttered a loud shriek, and hid her face in her hands; meanwhile her son ran right through the house, jumped into the court-yard, threw himself first into the kitchen garden and then into the flower garden, flew across the park into the road, and ran and ran, without once looking back, until at last he ceased to hear behind him the sound of his father's heavy feet, the loud and broken cries with which his father sobbed out, "Stop, villain! Stop, or I will curse you!"

Ivan Petrovich took refuge in the house of a neighbor,[A] and his father returned home utterly exhausted, and bathed in perspiration. There he announced, almost before he had given himself time to recover breath, that he withdrew his blessing and his property from his son, whose stupid books he condemned to be burnt; and he gave orders to have the girl Malania sent, with out delay, to a distant village. Some good people found out where Ivan Petrovich was, and told him everything. Full of shame and rage, he swore vengeance upon his father; and that very night, having lain in wait for the peasant's cart on which Malania was being sent away, he carried her off by force, galloped with her to the nearest town, and there married her. He was supplied with the necessary means by a neighbor, a hard-drinking, retired sailor, who was exceedingly good-natured, and a very great lover of all "noble histories," as he called them.

[Footnote A: Literally, "of a neighboring *Odnodvorets*." That word signifies one who belongs by descent to the class of nobles and proprietors, but who has no serfs belonging to him, and is really a moujik, or peasant. Some villages are composed of inhabitants of this class, who are often intelligent, though uneducated.]

The next day Ivan Petrovich sent his father a letter, which was frigidly and ironically polite, and then betook himself to the estate of two of his second cousins,—Dmitry Pestof, and his sister Marfa Timofeevna, with the latter of whom the reader is already acquainted. He told them everything that had happened, announced his intention of going to St. Petersburg to seek an appointment, and begged them to give shelter to his wife, even if only for a time. At the word "wife" he sobbed bitterly; and, in spite of his metropolitan education, and his philosophy, he humbly, like a thorough Russian peasant, knelt down at the feet of his relations, and even touched the floor with his forehead.

The Pestofs, who were kind and compassionate people, willingly consented to his request. With them he spent three weeks, secretly expecting an answer from his father. But no answer came; no answer could come. Peter Andreich, when he received the news of the marriage, took to his bed, and gave orders that his son's name should never again be mentioned to him; but Ivan's mother, without her husband's knowledge, borrowed five hundred paper roubles from a neighboring priest,[A] and sent them to her son, with a little sacred picture for his wife. She was afraid of writing, but she told her messenger, a spare little peasant who could walk sixty versts in a day, to say to Ivan that he was not to fret too much; that please God, all would yet go right, and his father's wrath would turn to kindness—that she, too, would have preferred a different daughter-in-law; but that evidently God had willed it as it was, and that she sent her paternal benediction to Malania Sergievna. The spare little peasant had a rouble given him, asked leave to see the new mistress, whose gossip[B] he was, kissed her hand, and returned home.

[Footnote A: Literally, "from the *Blagochinny*" an ecclesiastic who exercises supervision over a number of churches or parishes, a sort of Rural Dean.]

[Footnote A: The word is used in its old meaning of fellow-sponsor.]

So Ivan Petrovich betook himself to St. Petersburg with a light heart. An unknown future lay before him. Poverty might menace him; but he had broken with the hateful life in the country, and, above all, he had not fallen short of his instructors; he had really "put into action," and indeed done justice to, the doctrines of Rousseau, Diderot, and the "Declaration of the Rights of Man." The conviction of having accomplished a duty, a sense of pride and of triumph, filled his soul; and the fact of having to separate from his wife did not greatly alarm him; he would far sooner have been troubled by the necessity of having constantly to live with her. He had now to think of other affairs. One task was finished.

In St. Petersburg, contrary to his own expectations, he was successful. The Princess Kubensky—whom M. Courtin had already flung aside, but who had not yet contrived to die—in order that she might at least to some extent, make amends for her conduct towards her nephew, recommended him to all her friends, and gave him five thousand roubles—almost all the money she had left—and a watch, with his crest wrought on its back surrounded by a wreath of Cupids.

Three months had not gone by before he received an appointment on the staff of the Russian embassy in London, whither he set sail (steamers were not even talked about then) in the first homeward bound English vessel he could find. A few months later he received a letter from Pestof. The kind-hearted gentleman congratulated him on the birth of a son, who had come into the world at the village of Pokrovskoe, on the 20th of August, 1807, and had been named Fedor, in honor of the holy martyr Fedor Stratilates. On account of her extreme weakness, Malania Sergievna could add only a few lines. But even those few astonished Ivan Petrovich; he was not aware that Marfa Timofeevna had taught his wife to read and write.

It must not be supposed that Ivan Petrovich gave himself up for any length of time to the sweet emotion caused by paternal feeling. He was just then paying court to one of the celebrated Phrynes or Laises of the day—classical names were still in vogue at that time. The peace of Tilset was only just concluded,[A] and every one was hastening to enjoy himself, every one was being swept round by a giddy whirlwind. The black eyes of a bold beauty had helped to turn his head also. He had very little money, but he played cards luckily, made friends, joined in all possible diversions—in a word, he sailed with all sail set.

[Footnote A: In consequence of which the Russian embassy was withdrawn from London, and Ivan Petrovich probably went to Paris.]

Ivan S. Turgenev

IX

For a long time the old Lavretsky could not forgive his son
for his marriage. If, at the end of six months, Ivan Petrovich
had appeared before him with contrite mien, and had fallen
at his feet, the old man would, perhaps, have pardoned the
offender—after having soundly abused him, and given him a
tap with his crutch by way of frightening him. But Ivan
Petrovich went on living abroad, and, apparently, troubled
himself but little about his father. "Silence! don't dare to say
another word!" exclaimed Peter Andreich to his wife, every
time she tried to mollify him. "That puppy ought to be
always praying to God for me, since I have not laid my curse
upon him, the good-for-nothing fellow! Why, my late father
would have killed him with his own hands, and he would
have done well." All that Anna Pavlovna could do was to
cross herself stealthily when she heard such terrible words as
these. As to his son's wife, Peter Andreich would not so
much as hear of her at first; and even when he had to answer
a letter in which his daughter-in-law was mentioned by
Pestof, he ordered a message to be sent to him to say that he
did not know of any one who could be his daughter-in-law,
and that it was contrary to the law to shelter runaway female
serfs, a fact of which he considered it a duty to warn him.
But afterwards, on learning the birth of his grandson, his
heart softened a little; he gave orders that inquiries should be
secretly made on his behalf about the mother's health, and he

sent her—but still, not as if it came from himself—a small sum of money.

Before Fedor was a year old, his grandmother, Anna Pavlovna, was struck down by a mortal complaint. A few days before her death, when she could no longer rise from her bed, she told her husband in the presence of the priest, while her dying eyes swam with timid tears, that she wished to see her daughter-in-law, and to bid her farewell, and to bless her grandson. The old man, who was greatly moved, bade her set her mind at rest, and immediately sent his own carriage for his daughter-in-law, calling her, for the first time, Malania Sergievna.[A] Malania arrived with her boy, and with Marfa Timofeevna, whom nothing would have induced to allow her to go alone, and who was determined not to allow her to meet with any harm. Half dead with fright, Malania Sergievna entered her father-in-law's study, a nurse carrying Fedia behind her. Peter Andreich looked at her in silence. She drew near and took his hand, on which her quivering lips could scarcely press a silent kiss.

[Footnote A: That is to say, no longer speaking of her as if she were still a servant.]

"Well, noble lady,"[A] he said at last,—"Good-day to you; let's go to my wife's room."

[Footnote A: Literally "thrashed-while-damp noblewoman," *i.e.*, hastily ennobled. Much corn is thrashed in Russia before it has had time to get dry.]

He rose and bent over Fedia; the babe smiled and stretched out its tiny white hands towards him. The old man was touched.

"Ah, my orphaned one!" he said. "You have successfully

pleaded your father's cause. I will not desert you, little bird."

As soon as Malania Sergievna entered Anna Pavlovna's bed-room, she fell on her knees near the door. Anna Pavlovna, having made her a sign to come to her bedside, embraced her, and blessed her child. Then, turning towards her husband a face worn by cruel suffering, she would have spoken to him, but he prevented her.

"I know, I know what you want to ask," he said; "don't worry yourself. She shall remain with us, and for her sake I will forgive Vanka."[A]

[Footnote A: A diminutive of Ivan, somewhat expressive of contempt Vanya is the affectionate form.]

Anna Pavlovna succeeded by a great effort in getting hold of her husband's hand and pressing it to her lips. That same evening she died.

Peter Andreich kept his word. He let his son know that out of respect to his mother's last moments, and for the sake of the little Fedor, he gave him back his blessing, and would keep Malania Sergievna in his house. A couple of small rooms up-stairs were accordingly given to Malania, and he presented her to his most important acquaintances, the one-eyed Brigadier Skurekhine and his wife. He also placed two maid-servants at her disposal, and a page to run her errands.

After Marfa Timofeevna had left her—who had conceived a perfect hatred for Glafira, and had quarrelled with her three times in the course of a single day—the poor woman at first found her position difficult and painful. But after a time she attained endurance, and grew accustomed to her father-in-law. He, on his part, grew accustomed to her, and became fond of her, though he scarcely ever spoke to her, although in his caresses themselves a certain involuntary contempt showed itself. But it was her sister-in-law who made Malania suffer the most. Even during her mother's lifetime, Glafira had gradually succeeded in getting the entire management of the house into her own hands. Every one, from her father downwards, yielded to her. Without her permission not even a lump of sugar was to be got. She would have preferred to die rather than to delegate her authority to another housewife—and such a housewife too! She had been even more irritated than Peter Andreich by her brother's marriage, so she determined to read the upstart a good lesson, and from the very first Malania Sergievna became her slave. And Malania, utterly without defence, weak in health, constantly a prey to trouble and alarm—how could she have striven against the proud and strong-willed Glafira? Not a day passed without Glafira reminding her of her former position, and praising her for not forgetting herself. Malania Sergievna would willingly have acquiesced in these remindings and praisings, however bitter they might be—but her child had been taken away from her. This drove her to despair. Under the pretext that she was not qualified to see after his education, she was scarcely ever allowed to go near him. Glafira undertook the task. The child passed entirely into her keeping.

In her sorrow, Malania Sergievna began to implore her husband in her letters to return quickly. Peter Andreich himself wished to see his son, but Ivan Petrovich merely sent letters in reply. He thanked his father for what had been done for his wife, and for the money which had been sent to himself, and he promised to come home soon—but he did not come.

At last the year 1812 recalled him from abroad. On seeing each other for the first time after a separation of six years, the father and the son met in a warm embrace, and did not say a single word in reference to their former quarrels. Nor was it a time for that. All Russia was rising against the foe, and they both felt that Russian blood flowed in their veins, Peter Andreich equipped a whole regiment of volunteers at his own expense. But the war ended; the danger passed away. Ivan Petrovich once more became bored, once more he was allured into the distance, into that world in which he had grown up, and in which he felt himself at home. Malania could not hold him back; she was valued at very little in his eyes. Even what she really had hoped had not been fulfilled. Like the rest, her husband thought that it was decidedly most expedient to confide Fedia's education to Glafira. Ivan's poor wife could not bear up against this blow, could not endure this second separation. Without a murmur, at the end of a few days, she quietly passed away.

In the course of her whole life she had never been able to resist any thing; and so with her illness, also, she did not struggle. When she could no longer speak, and the shadows of death already lay on her face, her features still retained their old expression of patient perplexity, of unruffled and submissive sweetness. With her usual silent humility, she gazed at Glafira; and as Anna Pavlovna on her death-bed had kissed the hand of Peter Andreich, so she pressed her lips to Glafira's hand, as she confided to Glafira's care her only child. So did this good and quiet being end her earthly career. Like a shrub torn from its native soil, and the next moment flung aside, its roots upturned to the sun, she withered and disappeared, leaving no trace behind, and no one to grieve for her. It is true that her maids regretted her, and so did Peter Andreich. The old man missed her kindly face, her silent presence. "Forgive—farewell—my quiet one!" he said, as he took leave of her for the last time, in the church. He wept as he threw a handful of earth into her grave.

He did not long survive her—not more than five years. In the winter of 1819, he died peacefully in Moscow, whither he had gone with Glafira and his grandson. In his will he desired to be buried by the side of Anna Pavlovna and "Malasha."[A]

[Footnote A: Diminutive of Malania.]

Ivan Petrovich was at that time amusing himself in Paris, having retired from the service soon after the year 1815. On receiving the news of his father's death, he determined to return to Russia. The organization of his property had to be considered. Besides, according to Glafira's letter, Fedia had finished his twelfth year; and the time had come for taking serious thought about his education.

X

Ivan Petrovich returned to Russia an Anglomaniac. Short hair, starched frills, a pea-green, long-skirted coat with a number of little collars; a soar expression of countenance, something trenchant and at the same time careless in his demeanor, an utterance through the teeth, an abrupt wooden laugh, an absence of smile, a habit of conversing only on political or politico-economical subjects, a passion for under-done roast beef and port wine—every thing in him breathed, so to speak, of Great Britain. He seemed entirely imbued by its spirit. But strange to say, while becoming an Anglomaniac, Ivan Petrovich had also become a patriot,—at all events he called himself a patriot,—although he knew very little about Russia, he had not retained a single Russian habit, and he expressed himself in Russian oddly. In ordinary talk, his language was colorless and unwieldy, and absolutely bristled with Gallicisms. But the moment that the conversation turned upon serious topics, Ivan Petrovich immediately began to give utterance to such expressions as "to render manifest abnormal symptoms of enthusiasm," or "this is extravagantly inconsistent with the essential nature of circumstances," and so forth. He had brought with him some manuscript plans, intended to assist in the organization and improvement of the empire. For he was greatly discontented with what he saw taking place. It was the absence of system which especially aroused his indignation.

At his interview with his sister, he informed her in the first words he spoke that he meant to introduce radical reforms on his property, and that for the future all his affairs would be conducted on a new system. Glafira made no reply, but she clenched her teeth and thought, "What is to become of me then?" However, when she had gone with her brother and her nephew to the estate, her mind was soon set at ease. It is true that a few changes were made in the house, and the hangers-on and parasites were put to immediate flight. Among their number suffered two old women, the one blind, the other paralyzed, and also a worn-out major of the Ochakof[A] days, who, on account of his great voracity, was fed upon nothing but black bread and lentiles. An order was given also not to receive any of the former visitors; they were replaced by a distant neighbor, a certain blonde and scrofulous baron, an exceedingly well brought-up and remarkably dull man. New furniture was sent from Moscow; spittoons, bells, and washhand basins were introduced; the breakfast was served in a novel fashion; foreign wines replaced the old national spirits and liquors; new liveries were given to the servants, and to the family coat of arms was added the motto, "*In recto virtus.*"

[Footnote A: Ochakof is a town which was taken from the Turks by the Russians in 1788.]

In reality, however, the power of Glafira did not diminish; all receipts and expenditures were settled, as before, by her. A Valet, who had been brought from abroad, a native of Alsace, tried to compete with her, and lost his place, in spite of the protection which his master generally afforded him. In all that related to house-keeping, and also to the administration of the estate (for with these things too Glafira interfered)—in spite of the intention often expressed by Ivan Petrovich "to breathe new life into the chaos,"—all remained on the old footing. Only the *obrok*[A] remained on the old footing, and the *barshina*[B] became heavier, and the peasants were forbidden to go straight to Ivan Petrovich. The patriot already despised his fellow-citizens heartily. Ivan Petrovich's system was applied in its full development only to Fedia. The boy's education really underwent "a radical reform." His father undertook the sole direction of it himself.

[Footnote A: What the peasant paid his lord in money.]

[Footnote B: What the peasant paid his lord in labor.]

XI

Until the return of Ivan Petrovich from abroad, Fedia remained, as we have already said, in the hands of Glafira Petrovna. He was not yet eight years old when his mother died. It was not every day that he had been allowed to see her, but he had become passionately attached to her. His recollections of her, especially of her pale and gentle face, her mournful eyes, and her timid caresses, were indelibly impressed upon his heart. It was but vaguely that he understood her position in the house, but he felt that between him and her there existed a barrier which she dared not and could not destroy. He felt shy of his father, who, on his part, never caressed him. His grandfather sometimes smoothed his hair and gave him his hand to kiss, but called him a savage and thought him a fool. After Malania's death, his aunt took him regularly in hand. Fedia feared her, feared her bright sharp eyes, her cutting voice; he never dared to make the slightest noise in her presence; if by chance he stirred ever so little on his chair, she would immediately exclaim in her hissing voice, "Where are you going? sit still!"

On Sundays, after mass, he was allowed to play—that is to say, a thick book was given to him, a mysterious book, the work of a certain Maksimovich-Ambodik, bearing the title of "Symbols and Emblems." In this book there were to be found about a thousand, for the most part, very puzzling pictures, with equally puzzling explanations in five languages. Cupid, represented with a naked and chubby body, played a great part in these pictures. To one of them, the title of which was "Saffron and the Rainbow," was appended the explanation, "The effect of this is great." Opposite another, which represented "A Stork, flying with a violet in its beak," stood this motto, "To thee they are all known;" and "Cupid, and a bear licking its cub," was styled "Little by Little." Fedia used to pore over these pictures. He was familiar with them all even to their minutest details. Some of them—it was always the same ones—made him reflect, and excited his imagination: of other diversions he knew nothing.

When the time came for teaching him languages and music, Glafira Petrovna hired an old maid for a mere trifle, a Swede, whose eyes looked sideways, like a hare's, who spoke French and German more or less badly, played the piano so so, and pickled cucumbers to perfection. In the company of this governess, of his aunt, and of an old servant maid called Vasilievna, Fedia passed four whole years. Sometimes he would sit in a corner with his "Emblems"—there he would sit and sit. A scent of geraniums filled the low room, one tallow candle burnt dimly, the cricket chirped monotonously as if it were bored, the little clock ticked busily on the wall, a mouse scratched stealthily and gnawed behind the tapestry; and the three old maids, like the three Fates, knitted away silently and swiftly, the shadows of their hands now scampering along, now mysteriously quivering in the dusk; and strange, no less dusky, thoughts were being born in the child's mind.

No one would have called Fedia an interesting child. He was rather pale, but stout, badly built, and awkward—a regular moujik, to use the expression employed by Glafira Petrovna. The pallor would soon have vanished from his face if they had let him go out more into the fresh air. He learnt his lessons pretty well, though he was often idle. He never cried, but he sometimes evinced a savage obstinacy. At those times no one could do any thing with him. Fedia did not love a single one of the persons by whom he was surrounded. Alas for that heart which has not loved in youth!

Such did Ivan Petrovich find him when he returned; and, without losing time he at once began to apply his system to him.

"I want, above all, to make a man of him—*un homme*," he said to Glafira Petrovna "and not only a man, but a Spartan." This plan he began to carry out by dressing his boy in Highland costume. The twelve-year-old little fellow had to go about with bare legs, and with a cock's feather in his cap. The Swedish governess was replaced by a young tutor from Switzerland, who was acquainted with all the niceties of gymnastics. Music was utterly forbidden, as an accomplishment unworthy of a man. Natural science, international law, and mathematics, as well as carpentry, which was selected in accordance with the advice of Jean Jacques Rousseau; and heraldry, which was introduced for the maintenance of chivalrous ideas—these were the subjects to which the future "man" had to give his attention. He had to get up at four in the morning and take a cold bath immediately, after which he had to run round a high pole at the end of a cord. He had one meal a day, consisting of one dish; he rode on horseback, and he shot with a cross-bow. On every fitting occasion he had to exercise himself, in imitation of his father, in gaining strength of will; and every evening he used to write, in a book reserved for that purpose, an account of how he had spent the day, and what were his ideas on the subject. Ivan Petrovich, on his side, wrote instructions for him in French, in which he styled him *mon fils*, and addressed him as *vous*. Fedia used to say "thou" to his father in Russian, but he did not dare to sit down in his presence.

The "system" muddled the boy's brains, confused his ideas, and cramped his mind; but, as far as his physical health was concerned, the new kind of life acted on him beneficially. At first he fell ill with a fever, but he soon recovered and became a fine fellow. His father grew proud of him, and styled him in his curious language, "the child of nature, my creation." When Fedia reached the age of sixteen, Ivan Petrovich considered it a duty to inspire him in good time with contempt for the female sex—and so the young Spartan, with the first down beginning to appear upon his lips, timid in feeling, but with a body full of blood, and strength, and energy, already tried to seem careless, and cold, and rough.

Meanwhile time passed by. Ivan Petrovich spent the greater part of the year at Lavriki—that was the name of his chief hereditary estate; but in winter he used to go by himself to Moscow, where he put up at a hotel, attended his club assiduously, aired his eloquence freely, explained his plans in society, and more than ever gave himself out as an Anglomaniac, a grumbler, and a statesman. But the year 1825 came and brought with it much trouble[A]. Ivan Petrovich's intimate friends and acquaintances underwent a heavy tribulation. He made haste to betake himself far away into the country, and there he shut himself up in his house. Another year passed and Ivan Petrovich suddenly broke down, became feeble, and utterly gave way. His health having deserted him, the freethinker began to go to church, and to order prayers to be said for him[B]; the European began to steam himself in the Russian bath, to dine at two o'clock, to go to bed at nine, to be talked to sleep by the gossip of an old house-steward; the statesman burnt all his plans and all his correspondence, trembled before the governor, and treated the *Ispravnik*[C] with uneasy civility; the man of iron will whimpered and complained whenever he was troubled by a boil, or when his soup had got cold before he was served with it. Glafira again ruled supreme in the house; again did inspectors, overseers[D], and simple peasants begin to go up the back staircase to the rooms occupied by the "old witch"—as she was called by the servants of the house.

[Footnote A: Arising from the conspiracy of the "Decembrists" and their attempts at a revolution, on the occasion of the death of Alexander I., and the accession of Nicholas to the throne.]

[Footnote B: *Molebni*: prayers in which the name of the person who has paid for them is mentioned.]

[Footnote C: Inspector of rural police.]

[Footnote D: *Prikashchiki* and *Burmistrui*: two classes of overseers, the former dealing with economical matters only, the latter having to do with the administrative department also.]

The change which had taken place in Ivan Petrovich, produced a strong impression on the mind of his son. He had already entered on his nineteenth year; and he had begun to think for himself, and to shake off the weight of the hand which had been pressing him down. Even before this he had remarked how different were his father's deeds from his words; the wide and liberal theories he professed from the hard and narrow despotism he practiced; but he had not expected so abrupt a transformation. In his old age the egotist revealed himself in his full nature. The young Lavretsky was just getting ready to go to Moscow, with a view to preparing himself for the university, when a new and unexpected misfortune fell on the head of Ivan Petrovich. In the course of a single day the old man became blind, hopelessly blind.

Distrusting the skill of Russian medical men, he did all he could to get permission to travel abroad. It was refused. Then, taking his son with him, he wandered about Russia for three whole years, trying one doctor after another, incessantly journeying from place to place, and, by his impatient fretfulness, driving his doctors, his son, and his servants to the verge of despair. Utterly used up[A], he returned to Lavriki a weeping and capricious infant. Days of bitterness ensued, in which all suffered at his hands. He was quiet only while he was feeding. Never had he eaten so much, nor so greedily. At all other moments he allowed neither himself nor any one else to be at peace. He prayed, grumbled at fate, found fault with himself, with his system, with politics, with all which he used to boast of, with all that he had ever set up as a model for his son. He would declare that he believed in nothing, and then he would betake himself again to prayer; he could not bear a single moment of solitude, and he compelled his servants constantly to sit near his bed day and night, and to entertain him with stories, which he was in the habit of interrupting by exclamations of, "You're all telling lies!" or, "What utter nonsense!"

[Footnote A: Literally, "a regular rag."]

Glafira Petrovna had the largest share in all the trouble he gave. He was absolutely unable to do without her; and until the very end she fulfilled all the invalid's caprices, though sometimes she was unable to reply immediately to what he said, for fear the tone of her voice should betray the anger which was almost choking her. So he creaked on for two years more, and at length one day in the beginning of the month of May, he died. He had been carried out to the balcony, and planed there in the sun. "Glasha! Glashka! broth, broth, you old idi—," lisped his stammering tongue; and then, without completing the last word, it became silent forever. Glafira, who had just snatched the cup of broth from the hands of the major-domo, stopped short, looked her brother in the face, very slowly crossed herself, and went silently away. And his son, who happened also to be on the spot, did not say a word either, but bent over the railing of the balcony, and gazed for a long time into the garden, all green and fragrant, all sparkling in the golden sunlight of spring. He was twenty-three years old; how sadly, how swiftly had those years passed by unmarked! Life opened out before him now.

Ivan S. Turgenev

XII

After his father's burial, having confided to the never-changing Glafira Petrovna the administration of his household, and the supervision of his agents, the young Lavretsky set out for Moscow, whither a vague but powerful longing attracted him. He knew in what his education had been defective, and he was determined to supply its deficiencies as far as possible. In the course of the last five years he had read much, and he had see a good deal with his own eyes. Many ideas had passed through his mind, many a professor might have envied him some of his knowledge; yet, at the same time, he was entirely ignorant of much that had long been familiar to every school-boy. Lavretsky felt that he was not at his ease among his fellow-men; he had a secret inkling that he was an exceptional character. The Anglomaniac had played his son a cruel trick; his capricious education had borne its fruit. For many years he had implicitly obeyed his father; and when at last he had learned to value him aright, the effects of his father's teaching were already produced. Certain habits had become rooted in him. He did not know how to comport himself towards his fellow-men; at the age of twenty-three, with an eager longing after love in his bashful heart, he had not yet dared to look a woman in the face. With his clear and logical, but rather sluggish intellect, with his stubbornness, and his tendency towards inactivity and contemplation, he ought to have been flung at an early age into the whirl of life, instead of which he had been deliberately kept in seclusion. And now the magic circle was broken, but he remained standing on the same spot, cramped in mind and self-absorbed.

At his age it seemed a little ridiculous to put on the uniform of a student[A], but he did not fear ridicule. His Spartan education had at all events been so far useful, inasmuch as it had developed in him a contempt for the world's gossiping. So he donned a student's uniform without being disconcerted, enrolling himself in the faculty of physical and mathematical science. His robust figure, his ruddy face, his sprouting beard, his taciturn manner, produced a singular impression on his comrades. They never suspected that under the rough exterior of this man, who attended the lectures so regularly, driving up in a capacious rustic sledge, drawn by a couple of horses, something almost childlike was concealed. They thought him an eccentric sort of pedant, and they made no advances towards him, being able to do very well without him. And he, for his part, avoided them. During the first two years he passed at the university, he became intimate with no one except the student from whom she took lessons in Latin. This student, whose name was Mikhalevich, an enthusiast, and somewhat of a poet, grew warmly attached to Lavretsky, and quite accidentally became the cause of a serious change in his fortunes.

[Footnote A: The students at the Russian universities used to wear a uniform, but they no longer do so.]

One evening, when Lavretsky was at the theatre—he never missed a single representation, for Mochalof was then at the summit of his glory—he caught sight of a young girl in a box on the first tier. Never before had his heart beaten so fast, though at that time no woman ever passed before his stern eyes without sending its pulses flying. Leaning on the velvet

Ivan S. Turgenev

border of the box, the girl sat very still. Youthful animation lighted up every feature of her beautiful face; artistic feeling shone in her lovely eyes, which looked out with a soft, attentive gaze from underneath delicately pencilled eyebrows, in the quick smile of her expressive lips, in the bearing of her head, her arms, her neck. As to her dress, it was exquisite. By her side sat a sallow, wrinkled woman of five-and-forty, wearing a low dress and a black cap, with an unmeaning smile on her vacant face, to which she strove to give an aspect of attention. In the background of the box appeared an elderly man in a roomy coat, and with a high cravat. His small eyes had an expression of stupid conceit, modified by a kind of cringing suspicion; his mustache and whiskers were dyed, he had an immense meaningless forehead, and flabby cheeks: his whole appearance was that of a retired general.

Lavretsky kept his eyes fixed on the girl who had made such an impression on him. Suddenly the door of the box opened, and Mikhalevich entered. The appearance of the man who was almost his only acquaintance in all Moscow—his appearance in the company of the very girl who had absorbed his whole attention, seemed to Lavretsky strange and significant. As he continued looking at the box, he remarked that all its occupants treated Mikhalevich like an old friend. Lavretsky lost all interest in what was going on upon the stage; even Mochalof, although he was that evening "in the vein," did not produce his wonted impression upon him. During one very pathetic passage, Lavretsky looked almost involuntarily at the object of his admiration. She was leaning forward, a red glow coloring her cheeks. Her eyes were bent upon the stage, but gradually, under the influence of his fixed look, they turned and rested on him. All night long those eyes haunted him. At last, the carefully constructed dam was broken through. He shivered and he burnt by turns, and the very next day he went to see

Mikhalevich. From him he learned that the name of the girl he admired so much was Varvara Pavlovna Korobine, that the elderly people who were with her in the box were her father and her mother, and that Mikhalevich had become acquainted with them the year before, during the period of his stay as tutor in Count N.'s family, near Moscow. The enthusiast spoke of Varvara Pavlovna in the most eulogistic terms. "This girl, my brother," he exclaimed, in his peculiar, jerking kind of sing-song, "is an exceptional being, one endowed with genius, an artist in the true sense of the word, and besides all that, such an amiable creature." Perceiving from Lavretsky's questions how great an impression Varvara Pavlovna had made upon him, Mikhalevich, of his own accord, proposed to make him acquainted with her, adding that he was on the most familiar terms with them, that the general was not in the least haughty, and that the mother was as unintellectual as she well could be.

Lavretsky blushed, muttered something vague, and took himself off. For five whole days he fought against his timidity; on the sixth, the young Spartan donned an entirely new uniform, and placed himself at the disposal of Mikhalevich, who, as an intimate friend of the family, contented himself with setting his hair straight—and the two companions set off together to visit the Karobines.

XIII

Varvara Pavlovna's father, Pavel Petrovich Korobine, a retired major-general, had been on duty at St. Petersburg during almost the whole of his life. In his early years he had enjoyed the reputation of being an able dancer and driller; but as he was very poor he had to act as aide-de-camp to two or three generals of small renown in succession, one of whom gave him his daughter in marriage, together with a dowry of 25,000 roubles. Having made himself master of all the science of regulations and parades, even to their subtlest details, he "went on stretching the girth" until at last, after twenty years service, he became a general, and obtained a regiment. At that point he might have reposed, and have quietly consolidated his fortune. He had indeed counted upon doing so, but he managed his affairs rather imprudently. It seems he had discovered a new method of speculating with the public money. The method turned out an excellent one, but he must needs practise quite unreasonable economy,[A] so information was laid against him, and a more than disagreeable, a ruinous scandal ensued. Some how or other the general managed to get clear of the affair; but his career was stopped, and he was recommended to retire from active service. For about a couple of years he lingered on at St. Petersburg, in hopes that a snug civil appointment might fall to his lot; but no such appointment did fall to his lot. His daughter finished her education at the Institute; his expenses increased day by day. So he determined, with suppressed indignation, to go to Moscow for economy's sake; and there, in the Old Stable Street, he hired a little house with an escutcheon seven feet high on the roof, and began to live as retired generals do in Moscow on an income of 2,700 roubles a year[B].

[Footnote A: In other words, he stole, but he neglected to bribe.]

[Footnote B: Nearly L400, the roubles being "silver" ones. The difference in value between "silver" and "paper" roubles exists no longer.]

Moscow is an hospitable city, and ready to welcome any one who appears there, especially if he is a retired general. Pavel Petrovich's form, which, though heavy, was not devoid of martial bearing, began to appear in the drawing-rooms frequented by the best society of Moscow. The back of his head, bald, with the exception of a few tufts of dyed hair, and the stained ribbon of the Order of St. Anne, which he wore over a stock of the color of a raven's wing, became familiar to all the young men of pale and wearied aspect, who were wont to saunter moodily around the card tables while a dance was going on.

Pavel Petrovich understood how to hold his own in society. He said little, but always, as of old, spoke through the nose—except, of course, when he was talking to people of superior rank. He played at cards prudently, and when he was at home he ate with moderation. At a party he seemed to be feeding for six. Of his wife scarcely anything more can be said than that her name was Calliope Carlovna—that a tear always stood in her left eye, on the strength of which Calliope Carlovna, who to be sure was of German extraction, considered herself a woman of feeling—that she always

Ivan S. Turgenev

seemed frightened about something—that she looked as if she never had enough to eat—and that she always wore a tight velvet dress, a cap, and bracelets of thin, dull metal.

As to Varvara Pavlovna, the general's only daughter, she was but seventeen years old when she left the Institute in which she had been educated. While within its walls she was considered, if not the most beautiful, at all events the most intelligent of the pupils, and the best musician, and before leaving it she obtained the Cipher[A]. She was not yet nineteen when Lavretsky saw her for the first time.

[Footnote A: The initial letter of the name of the Empress, worn as a kind of decoration by the best pupils in the Imperial Institutes.]

XIV

The Spartan's legs trembled when Mikhalevich led him into the Korobines' not over-well furnished drawing-room, and introduced him to its occupants. But he overcame his timidity, and soon disappeared. In General Korobine that kindliness which is common to all Russians, was enhanced by the special affability which is peculiar to all persons whose fair fame has been a little soiled. As for the General's wife, she soon became as it were ignored by the whole party. But Varvara Pavlona was so calmly, so composedly gracious, that no one could be, even for a moment, in her presence without feeling himself at his ease. And at the same time from all her charming form, from her smiling eyes, from her faultlessly sloping shoulders, from the rose-tinged whiteness of her hands, from her elastic, but at the same time as it were, irresolute gait, from the very sound of her sweet and languorous voice—there breathed, like a delicate perfume, a subtle and incomprehensible charm—something which was at once tender and voluptuous and modest—something which it was difficult to express in words, which stirred the imagination and disturbed the mind, but disturbed it with sensations which were not akin to timidity.

Lavretsky introduced the subject of the theatre and the preceding night's performance; she immediately began to talk about Mochalof of her own accord, and did not confine herself

Ivan S. Turgenev

to mere sighs and exclamations, but pronounced several criticisms on his acting, which were as remarkable for sound judgment as for womanly penetration. Mikhalevich mentioned music; she sat down to the piano without affectation, and played with precision several of Chopin's mazurkas, which were then only just coming into fashion. Dinner time came. Lavretsky would have gone away, but they made him stop, and the General treated him at table with excellent Lafitte, which the footman had been hurriedly sent out to buy at Depre's.

It was late in the evening before Lavretsky returned home; and then he sat for a longtime without undressing, covering his eyes with his hand, and yielding to the torpor of enchantment. It seemed to him that he had not till now understood what makes life worth having. All his resolutions and intentions, all the now valueless ideas of other days, had disappeared in a moment. His whole soul melted within him into one feeling, one desire; into the desire of happiness, of possession, of love, of the sweetness of a woman's love.

From that day he began to visit the Korobines frequently. After six months had passed, he proposed to Varvara Pavlovna, and his offer was accepted. Long, long before, even if it was not the night before Lavretsky's first visit, the General had asked Mikhalevich how many serfs[A] his friend had. Even Varvara Pavlona, who had preserved her wonted composure and equanimity during the whole period of her young admirer's courtship, and even at the very moment of his declaration—even Varvara Pavlovna knew perfectly well that her betrothed was rich. And Calliope Carlovna thought to herself, "*Meine Tochter macht eine schoene Partie*[B]"—and bought herself a new cap.

[Footnote A: Literally, "souls," *i.e.*, male peasants.]

[Footnote B: My daughter is going to make a capital match.]

XV

And so his offer was accepted, but under certain conditions. In the first place, Lavretsky must immediately leave the university. Who could think of marrying a student? And what an extraordinary idea, a landed proprietor, a rich man, at twenty-six years of age, to be taking lessons like a schoolboy! In the second place, Varvara Pavlovna was to take upon herself the trouble of ordering and buying her trousseau. She even chose the presents the bridegroom was to give. She had very good taste, and a great deal of common sense, and she possessed a great liking for comfort, and no small skill in getting herself that comfort. Lavretsky was particularly struck by this talent when, immediately after the wedding, he and his wife set off for Lavriki, travelling in a convenient carriage which she had chosen herself. How carefully all their surroundings had been meditated over by Varvara Pavlovna! what prescience she had shown in providing them! What charming travelling contrivances made their appearance in the various convenient corners! what delicious toilet boxes! what excellent coffee machines! and how gracefully did Varvara Pavlovna herself make the coffee in the morning! But it must be confessed that Lavretsky was little fitted for critical observation just then. He revelled in his happiness, he was intoxicated by his good fortune, he abandoned himself to it like a child—he was, indeed, as innocent as a child, this young Hercules. Not in

Ivan S. Turgenev

vain did a charmed influence attach itself to the whole presence of his young wife; not in vain did she promise to the imagination a secret treasure of unknown delights. She was even better than her promise.

When she arrived at Lavriki, which was in the very hottest part of the summer, the house seemed to her sombre and in bad order, the servants antiquated and ridiculous; but she did not think it necessary to say a word about this to her husband. If she had intended to settle at Lavriki, she would have altered every thing there, beginning of course with the house; but the idea of staying in that out-of-the-way corner never, even for an instant, came into her mind. She merely lodged in it, as she would have done in a tent, putting up with all its discomforts in the sweetest manner, and laughing at them pleasantly.

When Marfa Timofeevna came to see her old pupil, she produced a favorable impression on Varvara Pavlovna. But Varvara was not at all to the old lady's liking. Nor did the young mistress of the house get on comfortably with Glafira Petrovna. She herself would have been content to leave Glafira in peace, but the general was anxious to get his hand into the management of his son-in-law's affairs. To see after the property of so near a relative, he said, was an occupation that even a general might adopt without disgrace. It is possible that Pavel Petrovich would not have disdained to occupy himself with the affairs of even an utter stranger.

Varvara Pavlovna carried out her plan of attack very skillfully. Although never putting herself forward, but being to all appearance thoroughly immersed in the bliss of the honeymoon, in the quiet life of the country, in music, and in books, she little by little worked upon Glafira, until that lady, one morning, burst into Lavretsky's study like a maniac, flung her bunch of keys on the table, and announced that she could no longer look after the affairs of the household, and that she did not wish to remain on the estate. As Lavretsky had been fitly prepared for the scene, he immediately gave his consent to her departure. This Glafira Petrovna had not expected. "Good," she said, and her brow grew dark. "I see that I am not wanted here. I know that I am expelled hence, driven away from the family nest. But, nephew, remember my words—nowhere will you be able to build you a nest; your lot will be to wander about without ceasing. There is my parting legacy to you." That same day she went off to her own little property: a week later General Korobine arrived, and, with a pleasantly subdued air, took the whole management of the estate into his own hands.

In September Varvara Pavlovna carried off her husband to St. Petersburg. There the young couple spent two winters—migrating in the summer to Tsarskoe Selo. They lived in handsome, bright, admirably-furnished apartments; they made numerous acquaintances in the upper and even the highest circles of society; they went out a great deal and received frequently, giving very charming musical parties and dances. Varvara Pavlovna attracted visitors as a light does moths.

Such a distracting life did not greatly please Fedor Ivanich. His wife wanted him to enter the service; but, partly in deference to his father's memory, partly in accordance with his own ideas, he would not do so, though he remained in St. Petersburg to please his wife. However, he soon found out that no one objected to his isolating himself, that it was not without an object that his study had been made the quietest and the most comfortable in the whole city, that his attentive wife was ever ready to encourage him in isolating himself; and from that time all went well. He again began to occupy himself with his as yet, as he thought, unfinished education. He entered upon anew course of reading; he even began the

Ivan S. Turgenev

study of English. It was curious to see his powerful, broad-shouldered figure constantly bending over his writing-table, his full, ruddy, bearded face, half-hidden by the leaves of a dictionary or a copy-book. His mornings were always spent over his work; later in the day he sat down to an excellent dinner—for Varvara Pavlovna always managed her household affairs admirably; and in the evening he entered an enchanted, perfumed, brilliant world, all peopled by young and joyous beings, the central point of their world being that extremely attentive manager of the household, his wife.

She made him happy with a son; but the poor child did not live long. It died in the spring; and in the summer, in accordance with the advice of the doctors, Lavretsky and his wife went the round of the foreign watering-places. Distraction was absolutely necessary for her after such a misfortune; and, besides, her health demanded a warmer climate. That summer and autumn they spent in Germany and Switzerland; and in the winter, as might be expected, they went to Paris.

In Paris Varvara Pavlovna bloomed like a rose; and there, just as quickly and as skilfully as she had done in St. Petersburg, she learnt how to build herself a snug little nest. She procured a very pretty set of apartments in one of the quiet but fashionable streets, she made her husband such a dressing-gown as he had never worn before; she secured an elegant lady's maid, an excellent cook, and an energetic footman; and she provided herself with an exquisite carriage, and a charming cabinet piano. Before a week was over she could already cross a street, put on a shawl, open a parasol, and wear gloves, as well as the most pure-blooded of Parisian women.

She soon made acquaintances also. At first only Russians

used to come to her house; then Frenchmen began to show themselves—amiable bachelors, of polished manners, exquisite in demeanor, and bearing high-sounding names. They all talked a great deal and very fast, they bowed gracefully, their eyes twinkled pleasantly. All of them possessed teeth which gleamed white between rosy lips; and how beautifully they smiled! Each of them brought his friends; and before long *La belle Madame de Lavretski* became well known from the *Chausee d' Antin* to the *Rue de Lille.* At that time—it was in 1836—the race of *feuilletonists* and journalists, which now swarms everywhere, numerous as the ants one sees when a hole is made in an ant-hill, had not yet succeeded in multiplying in numbers. Still, there used to appear in Varvara Pavlovna's drawing-room a certain M. Jules, a gentleman who bore a very bad character, whose appearance was unprepossessing, and whose manner was at once insolent and cringing—like that of all duellists and people who have been horsewhipped. Varvara disliked this M. Jules very much; but she received him because he wrote in several newspapers, and used to be constantly mentioning her, calling her sometimes Madame de L ... tski, sometimes Madame de * * *, *cette grande dame Russe si distinguee, qui demeure rue de P—*, and describing to the whole world, that is to say to some few hundreds of subscribers, who had nothing whatever to do with Madame de L ... tski, how loveable and charming was that lady, *une vraie francaise par l'esprit,*—the French have no higher praise than this,—what an extraordinary musician she was, and how wonderfully she waltzed. (Varvara Pavlovna did really waltz so as to allure all hearts to the skirt of her light, floating robe.) In fact, he spread her fame abroad throughout the world; and this we know, whatever people may say, is pleasant.

Mademoiselle Mars had by that time quitted the stage, and Mademoiselle Rachel had not yet appeared there; but for all that Varvara Pavlovna none the less assiduously attended the

Ivan S. Turgenev

theatres. She went into raptures about Italian music, and laughed over the ruins of Odry, yawned in a becoming manner at the legitimate drama, and cried at the sight of Madame Dorval's acting in some ultra-melodramatic piece. Above all, Liszt played at her house twice, and was so gracious, so unaffected! It was charming!

Amid such pleasurable sensations passed the winter, at the end of which Varvara Pavlovna was even presented at Court. As for Fedor Ivanovich, he was not exactly bored, but life began to weigh heavily on his shoulders at times—heavily because of its very emptiness. He read the papers, he listened to the lectures at the *Sorbonne* and the *College de France*, he followed the debates in the Chambers, he occupied himself in translating a famous scientific work on irrigation. "I am not wasting my time," he thought; "all this is of use; but next winter I really must return to Russia, and betake myself to active business." It would be hard to say if he had any clear idea of what were the special characteristics of that business, and only Heaven could tell whether he was likely to succeed in getting back to Russia in the winter. In the meanwhile he was intending to go with his wife to Baden. But an unexpected occurrence upset all his plans.

XVI

One day when he happened to go into Varvara Pavlovna's boudoir during her absence, Lavretsky saw a carefully folded little piece of paper lying on the floor. Half mechanically he picked it up and opened it—and read the following lines written in French:—

*   *   *   *   *

"MY DEAR ANGEL BETTY,

"(I really cannot make up my mind to call you Barbe or Varvara). I have waited in vain for you at the corner of the Boulevard. Come to our rooms to-morrow at half-past one. That excellent husband of yours is generally absorbed in his books at that time—we will sing over again that song of your poet Pushkin which you taught me, 'Old husband, cruel husband!' A thousand kisses to your dear little hands and feet. I await you.

"ERNEST."

*   *   *   *   *

At first Lavretsky did not comprehend the meaning of what he had read. He read it a second time—and his head swam, and the ground swayed beneath his feet like the deck of a ship in a storm, and a half-stifled sound issued from his lips, that was neither quite a cry nor quite a sob.

He was utterly confounded. He had trusted his wife so blindly; the possibility of deceit or of treachery on her part had never entered into his mind. This Ernest, his wife's lover, was a pretty boy of about three-and-twenty, with light hair, a turned-up nose, and a small moustache—probably the most insignificant of all his acquaintances.

Several minutes passed; a half hour passed. Lavretsky still stood there, clenching the fatal note in his hand, and gazing unmeaningly on the floor. A sort of dark whirlwind seemed to sweep round him, pale faces to glimmer through it.

A painful sensation of numbness had seized his heart. He felt as if he were falling, falling, falling—into a bottomless abyss.

The soft rustle of a silk dress roused him from his torpor by its familiar sound. Varvara Pavlovna came in hurriedly from out of doors. Lavretsky shuddered all over and rushed out of the room. He felt that at that moment he was ready to tear her to pieces, to strangle her with his own hands, at least to beat her all but to death in peasant fashion. Varvara Pavlovna, in her amazement, wanted to stay him. He just succeeded in whispering "Betty"—and then he fled from the house.

Lavretsky took a carriage and drove outside the barriers. All the rest of the day, and the whole of the night he wandered about, constantly stopping and wringing his hands above his head. Sometimes he was frantic with rage, at others every thing seemed to move him to laughter, even to a kind of mirth. When the morning dawned he felt half frozen, so he entered a wretched little suburban tavern, asked for a room, and sat down on a chair before the window. A convulsive fit of yawning seized him. By that time he was scarcely able to keep upright, and his bodily strength was utterly exhausted. Still he was not conscious of fatigue. But fatigue had its own way. He continued sitting there and gazing vacantly, but he comprehended nothing. He could not make out what had happened to him, why he found himself there, alone, in an empty, unknown room, with numbed limbs, with a sense of bitterness in his mouth, with a weight like that of a great stone on his heart. He could not understand what had induced her, his Varvara, to give herself to that Frenchman, and how, knowing herself to be false to him, she could have remained as calm as ever in his presence, as confiding and caressing as ever towards him. "I cannot make it out," whispered his dry lips. "And how can I be sure now that even at St. Petersburg—?" but he did not complete the question; a fresh gaping fit seized him, and his whole frame shrank and shivered. Sunny and sombre memories equally tormented him. He suddenly recollected how a few days before, she had sat at the piano, when both he and Ernest were present, and had sung "Old husband, cruel husband!" He remembered the expression of her face, the strange brilliance of her eyes, and the color in her cheeks—and he rose from his chair, longing to go to them and say, "You were wrong to play your tricks on me. My great grandfather used to hang his peasants on hooks by their ribs, and my grandfather was a peasant himself,"—and then kill them both. All of a sudden it would appear to him as if every thing that had happened were a dream, even not so much as a dream, but just some absurd fancy; as if he had only to give himself a shake and take a look round—and he did look round; and as a hawk claws a captured bird, so did his misery strike deeper and deeper into his heart. What made things worse was that Lavretsky had hoped, in the course of a few months, to find himself once more a father. His past, his future, his whole life was poisoned.

Ivan S. Turgenev

At last he returned to Paris, went to a hotel, and sent Varvara Pavlovna M. Ernest's note with the following letter:—

"The scrap of paper which accompanies this will explain every thing to you. I may as well tell you that you do not seem to have behaved in this matter with your usual tact. You, so careful a person, to drop such important papers (poor Lavretsky had been preparing this phrase, and fondling it, as it were, for several hours). I can see you no more, and I suppose that you too can have no wish for an interview with me. I assign you fifteen thousand roubles a year. I cannot give you more. Send your address to the steward of my estate. And now do what you like; live where you please. I wish you all prosperity. I want no answer."

Lavretsky told his wife that he wanted no answer; but he did expect, he even longed for an answer—an explanation of this strange, this incomprehensible affair. That same day Varvara Pavlovna sent him a long letter in French. It was the final blow. His last doubts vanished, and he even felt ashamed of having retained any doubts. Varvara Pavlovna did not attempt to justify herself. All that she wanted was to see him; she besought him not to condemn her irrevocably. The letter was cold and constrained, though marks of tears were to be seen on it here and there. Lavretsky smiled bitterly, and sent a message by the bearer, to the effect that the letter needed no reply.

Three days later he was no longer in Paris; but he went to Italy, not to Russia. He did not himself know why he chose Italy in particular. In reality, it was all the same to him where he went—so long as he did not go home. He sent word to his steward about his wife's allowance, ordering him, at the same time, to withdraw the whole management of the estate from General Korobine immediately, without waiting for any settlement of accounts, and to see to his Excellency's departure from Lavriki. He indulged in a vivid picture of the confusion of the expelled general, the useless airs which he would put on, and, in spite of his sorrow, he was conscious of a certain malicious satisfaction. At the same time he wrote to Glafira Petrovna, asking her to return to Lavriki, and drew up a power-of-attorney in her name. But Glafira Petrovna would not return to Lavriki; she even advertised in the newspapers that the power-of-attorney was cancelled,—a perfectly superfluous proceeding on her part.

Lavretsky hid himself in a little Italian town; but for a long time he could not help mentally following his wife's movements. He learned from the newspapers that she had left Paris for Baden, as she had intended. Her name soon appeared in a short article signed by the M. Jules of whom we have already spoken. The perusal of that article produced a very unpleasant effect on Lavretsky's mind. He detected in it, underneath the writer's usual sprightliness, a sort of tone of charitable commiseration. Next he learned that a daughter had been born to him. Two months later he was informed by his steward that Varvara Pavlovna had drawn her first quarter's allowance. After that, scandalous reports about her began to arrive; then they became more and more frequent; at last a tragicomic story, in which she played a very unenviable part, ran the round of all the journals, and created a great sensation. Affairs had come to a climax. Varvara Pavlovna was now "a celebrity."

Lavretsky ceased to follow her movements. But it was long before he could master his own feelings. Sometimes he was seized by such a longing after his wife, that he fancied he would have been ready to give every thing he had—that he could, perhaps, even have forgiven her—if only he might once more have heard her caressing voice, have felt once more her hand in his. But time did not pass by in vain. He was not born for suffering. His healthy nature claimed its

Ivan S. Turgenev

rights. Many things became intelligible for him. The very blow which had struck him seemed no longer to have come without warning. He understood his wife now. We can never fully understand persons with whom we are generally in close contact, until we have been separated from them. He was able to apply himself to business again, and to study, although now with much less than his former ardor; the scepticism for which both his education and his experience of life had paved the way, had taken lasting hold upon his mind. He became exceedingly indifferent to every thing. Four years passed by, and he felt strong enough to return to his home, to meet his own people. Without having stopped either at St. Petersburg or at Moscow, he arrived at O., where we left him, and whither we now entreat the reader to return with us.

XVII

About ten o'clock in the morning, on the day after that of which we have already spoken, Lavretsky was going up the steps of the Kalitines' house, when he met Liza with her bonnet and gloves on.

"Where are you going?" he asked her.

"To church. To-day is Sunday."

"And so you go to church?"

Liza looked at him in silent wonder.

"I beg your pardon," said Lavretsky. "I—I did not mean to say that. I came to take leave of you. I shall start for my country-house in another hour."

"That isn't far from here, is it?" asked Liza.

"About five-and-twenty versts."

At this moment Lenochka appeared at the door, accompanied by a maid-servant.

"Mind you don't forget us," said Liza, and went down

Ivan S. Turgenev

the steps.

"Don't forget me either. By the way," he continued, "you are going to church; say a prayer for me too, while you are there."

Liza stopped and turned towards him.

"Very well," she said, looking him full in the face. "I will pray for you, too. Come, Lenochka."

Lavretsky found Maria Dmitrievna alone in the drawing-room, which was redolent of Eau de Cologne and peppermint. Her head ached, she said, and she had spent a restless night.

She received him with her usual languid amiability, and by degrees began to talk.

"Tell me," she asked him, "is not Vladimir Nikolaevich a very agreeable young man?"

"Who is Vladimir Nikolaevich?"

"Why Panshine, you know, who was here yesterday. He was immensely delighted with you. Between ourselves I may mention, *mon cher cousin*, that he is perfectly infatuated with my Liza. Well, he is of good family, he is getting on capitally in the service, he is clever, and besides he is a chamberlain; and if such be the will of God—I, for my part, as a mother, shall be glad of it. It is certainly a great responsibility; most certainly the happiness of children depends upon their parents. But this much must be allowed. Up to the present time, whether well or ill, I have done every thing myself, and entirely by myself. I have brought up my children and taught them every thing myself—and now I have just written to Maclame Bulous for a governess—"

Maria Dmitrievna launched out into a description of her cares, her efforts, her maternal feelings. Lavretsky listened to her in silence, and twirled his hat in his hands. His cold, unsympathetic look at last disconcerted the talkative lady.

"And what do you think of Liza?" she asked.

"Lizaveta Mikhailovna is an exceedingly handsome girl," replied Lavretsky. Then he got up, said good-bye, and went to pay Marfa Timofeevna a visit. Maria Dmitrievna looked after him with an expression of dissatisfaction, and thought to herself, "What a bear! what a moujik! Well, now I understand why his wife couldn't remain faithful to him."

Marfa Timofeevna was sitting in her room, surrounded by her court. This consisted of five beings, almost equally dear to her heart—an educated bullfinch, to which she had taken an affection because it could no longer whistle or draw water, and which was afflicted with a swollen neck; a quiet and exceedingly timid little dog, called Roska; a bad-tempered cat, named Matros; a dark-complexioned, lively little girl of nine, with very large eyes and a sharp nose, whose name was Shurochka[A]; and an elderly lady of about fifty-five, who wore a white cap and a short, cinnamon-colored *katsaveika*[B] over a dark gown, and whose name was Nastasia Carpovna Ogarkof.

[Footnote A: One of the many diminutives of Alexandrina.]

[Footnote B: A kind of jacket worn by women.]

Shurochka was a fatherless and motherless girl, whose relations belonged to the lowest class of the bourgeoisie. Marfa Timofeevna had adopted her, as well as Roska, out of pity. She had found both the dog and the girl out in the streets. Both of them were thin and cold; the autumn rain had drenched them both. No one ever claimed Roska, and as to Shurochka, she was even gladly given up to Marfa Timofeevna by her uncle, a drunken shoemaker, who never had enough to eat himself, and could still less provide food for his niece, whom he used to hit over the head with his last.

As to Nastasia Carpovna, Marfa Timofeevna had made acquaintance with her on a pilgrimage, in a monastery. She went up to that old lady in church one day,—Nastasia Carpovna had pleased Marfa Timofeevna by praying as the latter lady said, "in very good taste"—began to talk to her, and invited her home to a cup of tea. From that day she parted with her no more. Nastasia Carpovna, whose father had belonged to the class of poor gentry, was a widow without children. She was a woman of a very sweet and happy disposition; she had a round head, grey hair, and soft, white hands. Her face also was soft, and her features, including a somewhat comical snub nose, were heavy, but pleasant. She worshipped Marfa Timofeevna, who loved her dearly, although she teased her greatly about her susceptible heart. Nastasia Carpovna had a weakness for all young men, and never could help blushing like a girl at the most innocent joke. Her whole property consisted of twelve hundred paper roubles.[A] She lived at Marfa Timofeevna's expense, but on a footing of perfect equality with her. Marfa Timofeevna could not have endured any thing like servility.

[Footnote A: About L50.]

"Ah, Fedia!" she began, as soon as she saw him

"You didn't see my family last night. Please to admire them now; we are all met together for tea. This is our second, our feast-day tea. You may embrace us all. Only Shurochka wouldn't let you, and the cat would scratch you. Is it to-day you go?"

"Yes," said Lavretsky, sitting down on a low chair. "I have just taken leave of Maria Dmitrievna. I saw Lizaveta Mikhailovna too."

"Call her Liza, my dear. Why should she be Mikhailovna for you? But do sit still, or you will break Shurochka's chair."

"She was on her way to church," continued Lavretsky. "Is she seriously inclined?"

"Yes, Fedia, very much so. More than you or I, Fedia."

"And do you mean to say you are not seriously inclined?" lisped Nastasia Carpovna. "If you have not gone to the early mass to-day, you will go to the later one."

"Not a bit of it. Thou shalt go alone. I've grown lazy, my mother," answered Marfa Timofeevna. "I am spoiling myself terribly with tea drinking."

She said *thou* to Nastasia Carpovna, although she lived on a footing of equality with her—but it was not for nothing that she was a Pestof. Three Pestofs occur in the Sinodik[A] of Ivan the Terrible. Marfa Timofeevna was perfectly well aware of the fact.

[Footnote A: "*I.e.*, in the list of the nobles of his time, in the sixteenth century.]

"Tell me, please," Lavretsky began again. "Maria Dmitrievna was talking to me just now about that—what's his name?— Panshine. What sort of a man is he?"

"Good Lord! what a chatter-box she is!" grumbled Marfa Timofeevna. "I've no doubt she has communicated to you as a secret that he hangs about here as a suitor. She might have been contented to 'Whisper about it with her *popovich*[A] But no, it seems that is not enough for her. And yet there is nothing settled so far, thank God! but she's always chattering."

[Footnote A: The priest's son. *i.e.*, Gedeonovsky.]

"Why do you say 'Thank God?'" asked Lavretsky.

"Why, because this fine young man doesn't please me. And what is there in the matter to be delighted about, I should like to know?"

"Doesn't he please you?"

"No; he can't fascinate every one. It's enough for him that Nastasia Carpovna here is in love with him."

The poor widow was terribly disconcerted.

"How can you say so, Marfa Timofeevna? Do not you fear God?" she exclaimed, and a blush instantly suffused her face and neck.

"And certainly the rogue knows how to fascinate her," broke in Marfa Timofeevna. "He has given her a snuff-box. Fedia, ask her for a pinch of snuff. You will see what a splendid snuff-box it is. There is a hussar on horseback on the lid. You had much better not try to exculpate yourself, my mother."

Nastasia Carpovna could only wave her hands with a deprecatory air.

"Well, but about Liza?" asked Lavretsky. "Is he indifferent to her?"

"She seems to like him—and as to the rest, God knows. Another person's heart, you know, is a dark forest, and more especially a young girl's. Look at Shurochka there! Come and analyze her's. Why has she been hiding herself, but not going away, ever since you came in?"

Shurochka burst into a laugh she was unable to stifle, and ran out of the room. Lavretsky also rose from his seat.

"Yes," he said slowly; "one cannot fathom a girl's heart."

As he was going to take leave.

"Well; shall we see you soon?" asked Marfa Timofeevna.

"Perhaps, aunt. It's no great distance to where I'm going."

"Yes; you're going, no doubt, to Vasilievskoe. You won't live at Lavriki. Well, that's your affair. Only go and kneel down at your mother's grave, and your grandmother's, too, while you are there. You have picked up all kinds of wisdom abroad there, and perhaps, who can tell, they may feel, even in their graves, that you have come to visit them. And don't forget, Fedia, to have a service said for Glafira Petrovna, too. Here is a rouble for you. Take it, take it please; it is I who wish to have the service performed for her. I didn't love her while she lived, but it must be confessed that she was a girl of character. She was clever. And then she didn't hurt you. And now go, and God be with you—else I shall tire you."

And Marfa Timofeevna embraced her nephew.

"And Liza shall not marry Panshine; don't make yourself

uneasy about that. He isn't the sort of man she deserves for a husband."

"But I am not in the least uneasy about it," remarked Lavretsky as he retired.

XVIII

Four hours later he was on his way towards his home. His tarantass rolled swiftly along the soft cross-road. There had been no rain for a fortnight. The atmosphere was pervaded by a light fog of milky hue, which hid the distant forests from sight, while a smell or burning filled the air. A number of dusky clouds with blurred outlines stood out against a pale blue sky, and lingered, slowly drawn. A strongish wind swept by in an unbroken current, bearing no moisture with it, and not dispelling the great heat. His head leaning back on the cushions, his arms folded across his breast, Lavretsky gazed at the furrowed plains which opened fanwise before him, at the cytisus shrubs, at the crows and rooks which looked sideways at the passing carriage with dull suspicion, at the long ridges planted with mugwort, wormwood, and mountain ash. He gazed—and that vast level solitude, so fresh and so fertile, that expanse of verdure, and those sweeping slopes, the ravines studded with clumps of dwarfed oaks, the grey hamlets, the thinly-clad birch trees—all this Russian landscape, so-long by him unseen, filled his mind with feelings which were sweet, but at the same time almost sad, and gave rise to a certain heaviness of heart, but one which was more akin to a pleasure than to a pain. His thoughts wandered slowly past, their forms as dark and ill-defined as those of the clouds, which also seemed vaguely wandering there on high. He thought of his childhood, of his

Ivan S. Turgenev

mother, how they brought him to her 011 her death-bed, and how, pressing his head to her breast, she began to croon over him, but looked up at Glafira Petrovna and became silent. He thought of his father, at first robust, brazen-voiced, grumbling at every thing—then blind, querulous, with white, uncared-for beard. He remembered how one day at dinner, when he had taken a little too much wine, the old man suddenly burst out laughing, and began to prate about his conquests, winking his blind eyes the while, and growing red in the face. He thought of Varvara Pavlovna—and his face contracted involuntarily, like that of a man who feels some sudden pain, and he gave his head an impatient toss. Then his thoughts rested on Liza. "There," he thought, "is a new life just beginning. A good creature! I wonder what will become of her. And she's pretty, too, with her pale, fresh face, her eyes and lips so serious, and that frank and guileless way she has of looking at you. It's a pity she seems a little enthusiastic. And her figure is good, and she moves about lightly, and she has a quiet voice. I like her best when she suddenly stands still, and listens attentively and gravely, then becomes contemplative and shakes her hair back. Yes, I agree, Panshine isn't worthy of her. Yet what harm is there in him? However, as to all that, why am I troubling my head about it? She will follow the same road that all others have to follow. I had better go to sleep." And Lavretsky closed his eyes.

He could not sleep, but he sank into a traveller's dreamy reverie. Just as before, pictures of by-gone days slowly rose and floated across his mind, blending with each other, and becoming confused with other scenes. Lavretsky began to think—heaven knows why—about Sir Robert Peel; then about French history; lastly, about the victory which he would have gained if he had been a general. The firing and the shouting rang in his ears. His head slipped on one side; he opened his eyes—the same fields stretched before him, the same level views met his eyes. The iron shoes of the outside horses gleamed brightly by turns athwart the waving dust, the driver's yellow[A] shirt swelled with the breeze. "Here I am, returning virtuously to my birth-place," suddenly thought Lavretsky, and he called out, "Get on there!" drew his cloak more closely around him, and pressed himself still nearer to the cushion. The tarantass gave a jerk. Lavretsky sat upright and opened his eyes wide. On the slope before him extended a small village. A little to the right was to be seen an old manor house of modest dimensions, its shutters closed, its portico awry. On one side stood a barn built of oak, small, but well preserved. The wide court-yard was entirely overgrown by nettles, as green and thick as hemp. This was Vasilievskoe.

[Footnote A: Yellow, with red pieces let in under the armpits.]

The driver turned aside to the gate, and stopped his horses. Lavretsky's servant rose from his seat, ready to jump down, and shouted "Halloo!" A hoarse, dull barking arose in reply, but no dog made its appearance. The lackey again got ready to descend, and again cried "Halloo!" The feeble barking was repeated, and directly afterwards a man, with snow-white hair, dressed in a nankeen caftan, ran into the yard from one of the comers. He looked at the tarantass, shielding his eyes from the sun, then suddenly struck both his hands upon his thighs, fidgeted about nervously for a moment, and finally ran to open the gates. The tarantass entered the court-yard, crushing the nettles under its wheels, and stopped before the portico. The white-headed old man, who was evidently of a very active turn, was already standing on the lowest step, his legs spread awkwardly apart. He unbuttoned the apron of the carriage, pulling up the leather with a jerk, and kissed his master's hand while assisting him to alight.

"Good day, good day, brother," said Lavretsky. "Your name is Anton, isn't it. So you're still alive?"

The old man bowed in silence, and then ran to fetch the keys. While he ran, the driver sat motionless, leaning sideways and looking at the closed door; and Lavretsky's man-servant remained in the picturesque attitude in which he found himself after springing clown to the ground, one of his arms resting on the box seat. The old man brought the keys and opened the door, lifting his elbows high the while, and needlessly wriggling his body—then he stood on one side, and again bowed down to his girdle.

"Here I am at home, actually returned!" thought Lavretsky, as he entered the little vestibule, while the shutters opened, one after another, with creak and rattle, and the light of day penetrated into the long-deserted rooms.

XIX

The little house at which Lavretsky had arrived, and in which Glafira Petrovna had died two years before, had been built of solid pine timber in the preceding century. It looked very old, but it was good for another fifty years or more. Lavretsky walked through all the rooms, and, to the great disquiet of the faded old flies which clung to the cornices without moving, their backs covered with white dust, he had the windows thrown open everywhere. Since the death of Glafira Petrovna, no one had opened them. Every thing had remained precisely as it used to be in the house. In the drawing-room the little white sofas, with their thin legs, and their shining grey coverings, all worn and rumpled, vividly recalled to mind the times of Catharine. In that room also stood the famous arm-chair of the late proprietress, a chair with a high, straight back, in which, even in her old age, she used always to sit bolt upright. On the wall hung an old portrait of Fedor's great-grandfather, Andrei Lavretsky. His dark, sallow countenance could scarcely be distinguished against the cracked and darkened background. His small, malicious eyes looked out morosely from beneath the heavy, apparently swollen eyelids. His black hair, worn without powder, rose up stiff as a brush above his heavy, wrinkled forehead. From the corner of the portrait hung a dusky wreath of *immortelles*. "Glafira Petrovna deigned to weave it herself," observed Anthony. In the bed-room stood a narrow bedstead, with curtains of some striped material, extremely old, but of very good quality. On the bed lay a heap of faded cushions and a thin, quilted counterpane; and above the bolster hung a picture of the Presentation of the Blessed Virgin in the Temple, the very picture which the old lady, when she lay dying, alone and forgotten, pressed for the last time with lips which were already beginning to grow cold. Near the window stood a toilet table, inlaid with different kinds of wood and ornamented with plates of copper, supporting a crooked mirror in a frame of which the gilding had turned black. In a line with the bed-room was the oratory, a little room with bare walls; in the corner stood a heavy case for holding sacred pictures, and on the floor lay the scrap of carpet, worn threadbare, and covered with droppings from wax candles, on which Glafira Petrovna used to prostrate herself when she prayed.

Anton went out with Lavretsky's servant to open the stable and coach-house doors. In his stead appeared an old woman, almost as old as himself, her hair covered by a handkerchief, which came down to her very eyebrows. Her head shook and her eyes seemed dim; but they wore, also, an expression of zealous obedience, habitual and implicit, and, at the same time, of a kind of respectful condolence. She kissed Lavretsky's hand, and then remained near the door, awaiting his orders. He could not remember what her name was, nor even whether he had ever seen her before. It turned out that her name was Apraxia. Some forty years previously, Glafira Petrovna had struck her off the list of the servants who lived in the house, and had ordered her to become a poultry-maid. She seldom spoke, seemed half idiotic, and always wore a servile look. Besides this old couple, and three paunchy little children in long shirts, Anton's great-grandchildren, there lived also in the seigniorial household an untaxable[A] moujik, who had only one arm. He cackled like a black-cock, and was fit for nothing. Of very little more use was the infirm old hound which had saluted Lavretsky's return by its barking. For ten whole years it had been fastened to a heavy chain, purchased by order of Glafira Petrovna, a burden under which it was now scarcely able to move.

[Footnote A: One who had not received the usual grant of land from the community, and was not subject to rates like the rest.]

Having examined the house, Lavretsky went out into the garden, and was well pleased with it. It was all overgrown with steppe grass, with dandelions, and with gooseberry and raspberry bushes; but there was plenty of shade in it, a number of old lime-trees growing there, of singularly large stature, with eccentrically ordered branches. They had been planted too close together, and a hundred years seemed to have elapsed since they were pruned. At the end of the garden was a small, clear lake, surrounded by a fringe of high, reddish-colored rushes. The traces of a human life that is past soon disappear. Glafira's manor-house had not yet grown wild, but it seemed to have become already immersed in that quiet slumber which all that is earthly sleeps, whenever it is not affected by the restlessness of humanity.

Lavretsky also went through the village. The women looked at him from the door-ways of their cottages, each resting her cheek upon her hand. The men bowed low from afar, the children ran Out of sight, the dogs barked away at their ease. At last he felt hungry, but he did not expect his cook and the other servants till the evening. The waggon bringing provisions from Lavriki had not yet arrived. It was necessary to have recourse to Anton. The old man immediately made his arrangements. He caught an ancient fowl, and killed and plucked it. Apraxia slowly squeezed and washed it, scrubbing it as if it had been linen for the wash, before putting it into the stewpan. When at last it was ready, Anton laid the table, placing beside the dish a three-footed plated salt-cellar, blackened with age, and a cut glass decanter, with a round glass stopper in its narrow neck. Then, in a kind of chant, he announced to Lavretsky that dinner was ready, and took his place behind his master's chair, a napkin wound around his right hand, and a kind of air of the past, like the odor of cypress-wood hanging about him. Lavretsky tasted the broth, and took the fowl out of it. The bird's skin was covered all over with round blisters, a thick tendon ran up each leg, and the flesh was as tough as wood, and had a flavor like that which pervades a laundry. After dinner Lavretsky said that he would take tea if—

"I will bring it in a moment," broke in the old man, and he kept his promise. A few pinches of tea were found rolled up in a scrap of red paper. Also a small, but very zealous and noisy little *samovar*[A] was discovered, and some sugar in minute pieces, which looked as if they had been all but melted away. Lavretsky drank his tea out of a large cup. From his earliest childhood he remembered this cup, on which playing cards were painted, and from which only visitors were allowed to drink; and now he drank from it, like a visitor.

[Footnote A: Urn.]

Towards the evening came the servants. Lavretsky did not like to sleep in his aunt's bed, so he had one made up for him in the dining-room. After putting out the candle, he lay for a long time looking around him, and thinking what were not joyous thoughts. He experienced the sensations which every one knows who has had to spend the night for the first time in a long uninhabited room. He fancied that the darkness which pressed in upon him from all sides could not accustom itself to the new tenant—that the very walls of the house were astonished at him. At last he sighed, pulled the counterpane well over him, and went to sleep. Anton remained on his legs long after every one else had gone to bed. For some time he spoke in a whisper to Apraxia, sighing low at intervals, and three times he crossed himself. The old servants had never expected that their master would settle down among them at Vasilievskoe, when he had such a fine estate, with a well-appointed manor-house close by. They did not suspect what was really the truth, that Lavriki was repugnant to its owner, that it aroused in his mind too painful recollections. After they had whispered to each other enough, Anton took a stick, and struck the watchman's board, which had long hung silently by the barn. Then he lay down in the open yard, without troubling himself about any covering for his white head. The May night was calm and soothing, and the old man slept soundly.

XX

The next day Lavretsky rose at a tolerably early hour, chatted with the *starosta*,[A] visited the rick-yard, and had the chain taken off the yard dog, which just barked a little, but did not even come out of its kennel. Then, returning home, he fell into a sort of quiet reverie, from which he did not emerge all day. "Here I am, then, at the very bottom of the river!"[B] he said to himself more than once. He sat near the window without stirring, and seemed to listen to the flow of the quiet life which surrounded him, to the rare sounds which came from the village solitude. Behind the nettles some one was singing with a thin, feeble voice; a gnat seemed to be piping a second to it The voice stopped, but the gnat still went on piping. Through the monotonous and obtrusive buzzing of the flies might be heard the humming of a large humble bee, which kept incessantly striking its head against the ceiling. A cock crowed in the street, hoarsely protracting its final note, a cart rattled past, a gate creaked in the village. "What?" suddenly screeched a woman's voice. "Ah, young lady!" said Anton to a little girl of two years old whom he was carrying in his arms. "Bring the *kvass* here," continued the same woman's voice. Then a death-like silence suddenly ensued.

[Footnote A: The head of the village.]

[Footnote B: A popular phrase, to express a life quiet as the depths of a river are.]

Nothing stirred, not a sound was audible. The wind did not move the leaves. The swallows skimmed along he ground one after another without a cry, and their silent flight made a sad impression upon the heart of the looker-on. "Here I am, then, at the bottom of the river," again thought Lavretsky. "And here life is always sluggish and still; whoever enters its circle must resign himself to his fate. Here there is no use in agitating oneself, no reason why one should give oneself trouble. He only will succeed here who traces his onward path as patiently as the plougher traces the furrow with his plough. And what strength there is in all around; what robust health dwells in the midst of this inactive stillness! There under the window climbs the large-leaved burdock from the thick grass. Above it the lovage extends its sappy stalk, while higher still the Virgin's tears hang out their rosy tendrils. Farther away in the fields shines the rye, and the oats are already in ear, and every leaf or its tree, every blade of grass on its stalk, stretches itself out to its full extent. On a woman's love my best years have been wasted!" (Lavretsky proceeded to think.) "Well, then, let the dulness here sober me and calm me down; let it educate me into being able to work like others without hurrying." And he again betook himself to listening to the silence, without expecting anything, and yet, at the same time, as if incessantly expecting something. The stillness embraced him on all sides; the sun went down quietly in a calm, blue sky, on which the clouds floated tranquilly, seeming as if they knew why and whither they were floating. In the other parts of the world, at that very moment, life was seething, noisily bestirring itself. Here the same life flowed silently along, like water over meadow grass. It was late in the evening before Lavretsky could tear himself away from the contemplation of this life so quietly welling forth—so tranquilly flowing past. Sorrow for the past melted away in his mind as the snow

Ivan S. Turgenev

melts in spring; but, strange to say, never had the love of home exercised so strong or so profound an influence upon him.

XXI

In the course of a fortnight Lavretsky succeeded in setting Glafira Petrovna's little house in order, and in trimming the court-yard and the garden. Its stable became stocked with horses; comfortable furniture was brought to it from Lavriki; and the town supplied it with wine, and with books and newspapers. In short, Lavretsky provided himself with every thing he wanted, and began to lead a life which was neither exactly that of an ordinary landed proprietor, nor exactly that of a regular hermit. His days passed by in uniform regularity, but he never found them dull, although he had no visitors. He occupied himself assiduously and attentively with the management of his estate; he rode about the neighborhood, and he read. But he read little. He preferred listening to old Anton's stories.

Lavretsky generally sat at the window, over a pipe and a cup of cold tea. Anton would stand at the door, his hands crossed behind his back, and would begin a deliberate narrative about old times, those fabulous times when oats and rye were sold, not By measure, but in large sacks, and for two or three roubles the sack; when on all sides, right up to the town, there stretched impenetrable forests and untouched steppes. "But now," grumbled the old man, over whose head eighty years had already passed, "everything has been so cut down and ploughed up that one can't drive anywhere." Anton would talk also at great length about his late mistress, Glafira Petrovna, saying how judicious and economical she was, how a certain gentleman, one of her young neighbors, had tried to gain her good graces for a time, and had begun to pay her frequent visits; and how in his honor she had deigned even to put on her gala-day cap with massacas ribbons, and her yellow dress made of *tru-tru-levantine*; but how, a little later, having become angry with her neighbor, that gentleman, on account of his indiscreet question, "I suppose, madam, you doubtless have a good sum of money in hand?" she told her servants never to let him enter her house again—and how she then ordered that, after her death, every thing, even to the smallest rag, should be handed over to Lavretsky. And, in reality, Lavretsky found his aunt's property quite intact, even down to the gala-day cap with the massacas ribbons, and the yellow dress of *tru-tru-levantine*.

As to the old papers and curious documents on which Lavretsky had counted, he found nothing of the kind except one old volume in which his grandfather, Peter Andreich, had made various entries. In one place might be read, "Celebration in the city of St. Petersburg, of the Peace concluded with the Turkish Empire by his Excellency, Prince Alexander Alexandrovich Prozorovsky". In another, "Recipe of a decoction for the chest," with the remark. "This prescription was given the Generaless Prascovia Fedorovna Saltykof, by the Archpresbyter of the Life-beginning Trinity, Fedor Avksentevich." Sometimes there occurred a piece of political information, as follows:—

"About the French tigers there is somehow silence"—and close by, "In the *Moscow Gazette* there is an announcement of the decease of the First-Major Mikhail Petrovich Kolychef. Is not this the son of Peter Vasilievich Kolychef?"

Lavretsky also found some old calendars and dream-books,

and the mystical work of M. Ambodik. Many a memory did the long-forgotten but familiar "Symbols and Emblems" recall to his mind. In the furthest recess of one of the drawers in Glafira's toilette-table, Lavretsky found a small packet, sealed with black wax, and tied with a narrow black ribbon. Inside the packet were two portraits lying face to face, the one, in pastel, of his father as a young man, with soft curls falling over his forehead, with long, languid eyes, and with a half-open mouth; the other an almost obliterated picture of a pale woman, in a white dress, with a white rose in her hand—his mother. Of herself Glafira never would allow a portrait to be taken.

"Although I did not then live in the house," Anton would say to Lavretsky, "yet I can remember your great grandfather, Andrei Afanasich. I was eighteen years old when he died. One day I met him in the garden—then my very thighs began to quake. But he didn't do anything, only asked me what my name was, and sent me to his bed-room for a pocket-handkerchief. He was truly a seigneur—every one must allow that; and he wouldn't allow that any one was better than himself. For I may tell you, your great grandfather had such a wonderful amulet—a monk from Mount Athos had given him that amulet—and that monk said to him, 'I give thee this, O Boyar, in return for thy hospitality. Wear it, and fear no judge.' Well, it's true, as is well known, that times were different then. What a seigneur wanted to do, that he did. If ever one of the gentry took it into his head to contradict him, he would just look at him, and say, 'Thou swimmest in shallow water'[A]—that was a favorite phrase with him. And he lived, did your great grandfather of blessed memory, in small, wooden rooms. But what riches he left behind him! What silver, what stores of all kinds! All the cellars were crammed full of them. He was a real manager. That little decanter which you were pleased to praise was his. He used to drink brandy out of it. But just see! your grandfather, Peter Andreich, provided himself with a stone mansion, but he lived worse than his father, and got himself no satisfaction, but spent all his money, and now there is nothing to remember him by—not so much as a silver spoon has come down to us from him; and for all that is left, one must thank Glafira Petrovna's care."

[Footnote A: Part of a Russian proverb.]

"But is it true," interrupted Lavretsky, "that people used to call her an old witch?"

"But, then, who called her so?" replied Anton, with an air of discontent.

"But what is our mistress doing now, *batyushka*?" the old man ventured to ask one day. "Where does she please to have her habitation?"

"I am separated from my wife," answered Lavretsky, with an effort. "Please don't ask me about her."

"I obey," sadly replied the old man.

At the end of three weeks Lavretsky rode over to O., and spent the evening at the Kalitines' house. He found Lemm there, and took a great liking to him. Although, thanks to his father, Lavretsky could not play any instrument, yet he was passionately fond of music—of classical, serious music, that is to say. Panshine was not at the Kalitines' that evening, for the Governor had sent him somewhere into the country. Liza played unaccompanied, and that with great accuracy. Lemm grew lively and animated, rolled up a sheet of paper, and conducted the music. Maria Dmitrievna looked at him laughingly for a while, and then went off to bed. According to her, Beethoven was too agitating for her nerves.

At midnight Lavretsky saw Lemm home, and remained with him till three in the morning. Lemm talked a great deal. He stooped less than usual, his eyes opened wide and sparkled, his very hair remained pushed off from his brow. It was so long since any one had shown any sympathy with him, and Lavretsky was evidently interested in him, and questioned him carefully and attentively. This touched the old man. He ended by showing his music to his guest, and he played, and even sang, in his worn-out voice, some passages from his own works; among others, an entire ballad of Schiller's that he had set to music—that of Fridolin. Lavretsky was loud in its praise, made him repeat several parts, and, on going away, invited him to spend some days with him. Lemm, who was conducting him to the door, immediately consented, pressing his hand cordially. But when he found himself alone in the fresh, damp air, beneath the just-appearing dawn, he looked round, half-shut his eyes, bent himself together, and crept back, like a culprit, to his bed-room. "*Ich bin wohl nicht klug*"—("I must be out of my wits"), he murmured, as he lay down on his short, hard bed.

He tried to make out that he was ill when, a few days later, Lavretsky's carriage came for him. But Lavretsky went up into his room, and persuaded him to go. Stronger than every other argument with him was the fact that Lavretsky had ordered a piano to be sent out to the country-house on purpose for him. The two companions went to the Kalitines' together, and spent the evening there, but not quite so pleasantly as on the previous occasion. Panshine was there, talking a great deal about his journey, and very amusingly mimicking the various proprietors he had met, and parodying their conversation. Lavretsky laughed, but Lemm refused to come out of his corner, where he remained in silence, noiselessly working his limbs like a spider, and wearing a dull and sulky look. It was not till he rose to take leave that he became at all animated. Even when sitting in the carriage,

Ivan S. Turgenev

the old man at first seemed still unsociable and absorbed in his own thoughts. But the calm, warm air, the gentle breeze, the dim shadows, the scent of the grass and the birch buds, the peaceful light of the moonless, starry sky, the rhythmical tramp and snorting of the horses, the mingled fascinations of the journey, of the spring, of the night—all entered into the soul of the poor German, and he began to talk with Lavretsky of his own accord.

XXII

He began to talk about music, then about Liza, and then again about music. He seemed to pronounce his words more slowly when he spoke of Liza. Lavretsky turned the conversation to the subject of his compositions, and offered, half in jest, to write a libretto for him.

"Hm! a libretto!" answered Lemm. "No; that is beyond me. I no longer have the animation, the play of fancy, which are indispensable for an opera. Already my strength has deserted me. But if I could still do something, I should content myself with a romance. Of course I should like good words."

He became silent, and sat for a long time without moving, his eyes fixed on the sky.

"For instance," he said at length, "something in this way—'O stars, pure stars!'"

Lavretsky turned a little, and began to regard him attentively.

"'O stars, pure stars!'" repeated Lemm, "'you look alike on the just and the unjust. But only the innocent of heart'—or something of that kind—'understand you'—that is to say, no—'love you.' However, I am not a poet. What am I thinking about! But something of that kind—something lofty."

Ivan S. Turgenev

Lemm pushed his hat back from his forehead. Seen by the faint twilight of the clear night, his face seemed paler and younger.

"'And you know also,'" he continued, in a gradually lowered voice, "'you know those who love, who know how to love; for you are pure, you alone can console.' No; all that is not what I mean. I am not a poet. But something of that kind."—

"I am sorry that I am not a poet either," remarked Lavretsky.

"Empty dreams!" continued Lemm, as he sank into the corner of the carriage. Then he shut his eyes as if he had made up his mind to go to sleep;

Several minutes passed. Lavretsky still listened.

"Stars, pure stars ... love'" whispered the old man.

"Love!" repeated Lavretsky to himself. Then he fell into a reverie, and his heart grew heavy within him.

"You have set 'Fridolin' to charming music, Christopher Fedorovich," he said aloud after a time. But what is your opinion? This Fridolin, after he had been brought into the presence of the countess by her husband, didn't he then immediately become her lover—eh?"

"You think so," answered Lemm, "because, most likely, experience—"

He stopped short, and turned away in confusion.

Lavretsky uttered a forced laugh. Then he too turned away from his companion, and began looking out along the road.

The stars had already begun to grow pale, and the sky to turn grey, when the carriage arrived before the steps of the little house at Vasilievskoe. Lavretsky conducted his guest to his allotted room, then went to his study, and sat down in front of the window. Out in the garden a nightingale was singing its last song before the dawn. Lavretsky remembered that at the Kalitines' also a nightingale had sung in the garden. He remembered also the quiet movement of Liza's eyes when, at its first notes, she had turned toward the dark casement. He began to think of her, and his heart grew calm.

"Pure maiden," he said, in a half-whisper, "pure stars," he added, with a smile, and then quietly lay down to sleep.

But Lemm sat for a long time on his bed, with a sheet of music on his knees. It seemed as if some sweet melody, yet unborn, were intending to visit him. He already underwent the feverish agitation, he already felt the fatigue and the delight, of its vicinity; but it always eluded him.

"Neither poet nor musician!" he whispered at last; and his weary head sank heavily upon the pillow.

*   *   *   *   *

The next morning Lavretsky and his guest drank their tea in the garden, under an old lime-tree.

"Maestro," said Lavretsky, among other things, "you will soon have to compose a festal cantata."

"On what occasion?"

"Why, on that of Mr. Panshine's marriage with Liza. Didn't you observe what attention he paid her yesterday? All goes smoothly with them evidently."

"That will never be!" exclaimed Lemm.

"Why?"

"Because it's impossible. However," he added after pausing awhile, "in this world everything is possible. Especially in this country of yours—in Russia."

"Let us leave Russia out of the question for the present. But what do you see objectionable in that marriage?"

"Every thing is objectionable—every thing. Lizaveta Mikhailovna is a serious, true-hearted girl, with lofty sentiments. But he—he is, to describe him by one word, a *dil-le-tante*"

"But doesn't she love him?"

Lemm rose from his bench.

"No, she does not love him. That is to say, she is very pure of heart, and does not herself know the meaning of the words, 'to love.' Madame Von Kalitine tells her that he is an excellent young man; and she obeys Madame Von Kalitine because she is still quite a child, although she is now nineteen. She says her prayers every morning; she says her prayers every evening—and that is very praiseworthy. But she does not love him. She can love only what is noble. But he is not noble; that is to say, his soul is not noble."

Lemm uttered the whole of this speech fluently, and with animation, walking backwards and forwards with short steps in front of the tea-table, his eyes running along the ground meanwhile.

"Dearest Maestro!" suddenly exclaimed Lavretsky, "I think

you are in love with my cousin yourself."

Lemm suddenly stopped short.

"Please do not jest with me in that way," he began, with faltering voice. "I am not out of my mind. I look forward to the dark grave, and not to a rosy future."

Lavretsky felt sorry for the old man, and begged his pardon. After breakfast Lemm played his cantata, and after dinner, at Lavretsky's own instigation, he again began to talk about Liza. Lavretsky listened to him attentively and with curiosity.

"What do you say to this, Christopher Fedorovitch?" he said at last. "Every thing seems in order here now, and the garden is in full bloom. Why shouldn't I invite her to come here for the day, with her mother and my old aunt—eh? Will that be agreeable to you?"

Lemm bowed his head over his plate.

"Invite her," he said, in a scarcely audible voice.

"But we needn't ask Panshine."

"No, we needn't," answered the old man, with an almost childlike smile.

Two days later Lavretsky went into town and to the Kalatines'.

XXIII

He found them all at home, but he did not tell them of his plan immediately. He wanted to speak to Liza alone first. Chance favored him, and he was left alone with her in the drawing-room. They began to talk. As a general rule she was never shy with any one, and by this time she had succeeded in becoming accustomed to him. He listened to what she said, and as he looked at her face, he musingly repeated Lemm's words, and agreed with him. It sometimes happens that two persons who are already acquainted with each other, but not intimately, after the lapse of a few minutes suddenly become familiar friends—and the consciousness of this familiarity immediately expresses itself in their looks, in their gentle and kindly smiles, in their gestures themselves. And this happened now with Lavretsky and Liza. "Ah, so that's what's you're like!" thought she, looking at him with friendly eyes. "Ah, so that's what's you're like!" thought he also; and therefore he was not much surprised when she informed him, not without some little hesitation, that she had long wanted to say something to him, but that she was afraid of vexing him.

"Don't be afraid, speak out," he said, standing still in front of her.

Liza raised her clear eyes to his.

"You are so good," she began—and at the same time she thought, "yes, he is really good"—"I hope you will forgive me. I scarcely ought to have ventured to speak to you about it—but how could you—why did you separate from your wife?"

Lavretsky shuddered, then looked at Liza, and sat down by her side.

"My child," he began to say, "I beg you not to touch upon that wound. Your touch is light, but—in spite of all that, it will give me pain."

"I know," continued Liza, as if she had not heard him, "that she is guilty before you. I do not want to justify her. But how can they be separated whom God has joined together?"

"Our convictions on that score are widely different, Lizaveta Mikhailovna," said Lavretsky, somewhat coldly. "We shall not be able to understand one another."

Liza grew pale. Her whole body shuddered slightly, but she was not silenced.

"You ought to forgive," she said quietly, "if you wish also to be forgiven."

"Forgive!" cried Lavretsky; you ought first to know her for whom you plead. Forgive that woman, take her back to my house, her, that hollow, heartless, creature! And who has told you that she wants to return to me? Why, she is completely satisfied with her position. But why should we talk of her? Her name ought never to be uttered by you. You are too pure, you are not in a position even to understand such a being."

"Why speak so bitterly?" said Liza, with an effort. The

trembling of her hands began to be apparent. "You left her of your own accord, Fedor Ivanich."

"But I tell you," replied Lavretsky, with an involuntary burst of impatience, "you do not know the sort of creature she is."

"Then why did you marry her?" whispered Liza, with downcast eyes.

Lavretsky jumped up quickly from his chair.

"Why did I marry her? I was young and inexperienced then. I was taken in. A beautiful exterior fascinated me. I did not understand women; there was nothing I did understand. God grant you may make a happier marriage! But take my word for it, it is impossible to be certain about anything."

"I also may be unhappy," said Liza, her voice beginning to waver, "but then I shall have to be resigned. I cannot express myself properly, but I mean to say that if we are not resigned—"

Lavretsky clenched his hands and stamped his foot.

"Don't be angry; please forgive me," hastily said Liza. At that moment Maria Dmitrievna came into the room. Liza stood up and was going away, when Lavretsky unexpectedly called after her:

"Stop a moment. I have a great favor to ask of your mother and you. It is that you will come and pay me a visit in my new home. I've got a piano, you know; Lemm is stopping with me; the lilacs are in bloom. You will get a breath of country air, and be able to return the same day. Do you consent?"

Liza looked at her mother, who immediately assumed an air

of suffering. But Lavretsky did not give Madame Kalatine time to open her mouth. He instantly took both of her hands and kissed them, and Maria Dmitrievna, who always responded to winning ways, and had never for a moment expected such a piece of politeness from "the bear," felt herself touched, and gave her consent. While she was considering what day to appoint, Lavretsky went up to Liza, and, still under the influence of emotion, whispered aside to her, "Thanks. You are a good girl. I am in the wrong." Then a color came into her pale face, which lighted up with a quiet but joyous smile. Her eyes also smiled. Till that moment she had been afraid that she had offended him.

"M. Panshine can come with us, I suppose?" asked Maria Dmitrievna.

"Of course," replied Lavretsky. "But would it not be better for us to keep to our family circle?"

"But I think—" began Maria Dmitrievna, adding, however, "Well, just as you like."

It was settled that Lenochka and Shurochka should go. Marfa Timofeevna refused to take part in the excursion.

"It's a bore to me, my dear," she said, "to move my old bones; and there's nowhere, I suppose, in your house where I could pass the night; besides, I never can sleep in a strange bed. Let these young folks caper as they please."

Lavretsky had no other opportunity of speaking with Liza alone, but he kept looking at her in a manner that pleased her, and at the same time confused her a little. She felt very sorry for him. When he went away, he took leave of her with a warm pressure of the hand. She fell into a reverie as soon as she found herself alone.

XXIV

[Footnote A: Omitted in the French translation.]

On entering the drawing-room, after his return home, Lavretsky met a tall, thin man, with a wrinkled but animated face, untidy grey whiskers, a long, straight nose, and small, inflamed eyes. This individual, who was dressed in a shabby blue surtout, was Mikhalevich, his former comrade at the University. At first Lavretsky did not recognize him, but he warmly embraced him as soon as he had made himself known. The two friends had not seen each other since the old Moscow days. Then followed exclamations and questions. Memories long lost to sight came out again into the light of day. Smoking pipe after pipe in a hurried manner, gulping down his tea, and waving his long hands in the air, Mikhalevich related his adventures. There was nothing very brilliant about them, and he could boast of but little success in his various enterprises; but he kept incessantly laughing a hoarse, nervous laugh. It seemed that about a month previously he had obtained a post in the private counting-house of a rich brandy-farmer,[A] at about three hundred versts from O., and having heard of Lavretsky's return from abroad, he had turned out of his road for the purpose of seeing his old friend again. He spoke just as jerkingly as he used to do in the days of youth, and he became as noisy and as warm as he was in the habit of growing then. Lavretsky began to speak about his own affairs, but Mikhalevich stopped him, hastily stammering out, "I have heard about it, brother; I have heard about it. Who could have expected it?" and then immediately turned the conversation on topics of general interest.

[Footnote A: One of the contractors who used to purchase the right of supplying the people with brandy.]

"I must go away again to-morrow, brother," he said. "To-day, if you will allow it, we will sit up late. I want to get a thoroughly good idea of what you are now, what your intentions are and your convictions, what sort of man you have become, what life has taught you" (Mikhalevich still made use of the phraseology current in the year 1830). "As for me, brother, I have become changed in many respects. The waters of life have gone over my breast. Who was it said that? But in what is important, what is substantial, I have not changed. I believe, as I used to do, in the Good, in the True. And not only do I believe, but I feel certain now—yes, I feel certain, certain. Listen; I make verses, you know. There's no poetry in them, but there is truth. I will read you my last piece. I have expressed in it my most sincere convictions. Now listen."

Mikhalevich began to read his poem, which was rather a long one. It ended with the following lines:—

"With my whole heart have I given myself up to new feelings;
In spirit I have become like unto a child,
And I have burnt all that I used to worship,
I worship all that I used to burn."

Mikhalevich all but wept as he pronounced these last two verses. A slight twitching, the sign of a strong emotion, affected his large lips; his plain face lighted up. Lavretsky went on listening until at last the spirit of contradiction was roused within him. He became irritated by the Moscow student's enthusiasm, so perpetually on the boil, so continually ready for use. A quarter of an hour had not elapsed before a dispute had been kindled between the two friends, one of those endless disputes of which only Russians are capable. They two, after a separation which had lasted for many years, and those passed in two different worlds, neither of them clearly understanding the other's thoughts, not even his own, holding fast by words, and differing in words alone, disputed about the most purely abstract ideas—and disputed exactly as if the matter had been one of life and death to both of them. They shouted and cried aloud to such an extent that every one in the house was disturbed, and poor Lemm, who had shut himself up in his room the moment Mikhalevich arrived, felt utterly perplexed, and even began to entertain some vague form of fear.

"But after all this, what are you? *blasé*!"[A] cried Mikhalevich at midnight.

[Footnote A: Literally, "disillusioned."]

"Does a *blasé* man ever look like me?" answered Lavretsky. "He is always pale and sickly; but I, if you like, will lift you off the ground with one hand."

"Well then, if not *blasé*, at least a sceptic,[A] and that is still worse. But what right have you to be a sceptic? Your life has not been a success, I admit. That wasn't your fault. You were endowed with a soul full of affection, fit for passionate love, and you were kept away from women by force. The first woman you came across was sure to take you in."

[Footnote A: He says in that original *Skyeptuik* instead of

Skeptik, on which the author remarks, "Mikhalevich's accent testified to his birth-place having been in Little Russia."]

"She took you in, too," morosely remarked Lavretsky.

"Granted, granted. In that I was the tool of fate. But I'm talking nonsense. There's no such thing as fate. My old habit of expressing myself inaccurately! But what does that prove?"

"It proves this much, that I have been distorted from childhood."

"Well, then, straighten yourself. That's the good of being a man. You haven't got to borrow energy. But, however that may be, is it possible, is it allowable, to work upwards from an isolated fact, so to speak, to a general law—to an invariable rule?"

"What rule?" said Lavretsky, interrupting him. "I do not admit—"

"No, that is your rule, that is your rule," cried the other, interrupting him in his turn.

"You are an egotist, that's what it is!" thundered Mikhalevich an hour later. "You wanted self-enjoyment; you wanted a happy life; you wanted to live only for yourself—"

"What is self-enjoyment?"

"—And every thing has failed you; everything has given way under your feet."

"But what is self-enjoyment, I ask you?"

Ivan S. Turgenev

"—And it ought to give way. Because you looked for support there, where it is impossible to find it; because you built your house on the quicksands—"

"Speak plainer, without metaphor, *because* I do not understand you."

"—Because—laugh away if you like—because there is no faith in you, no hearty warmth—and only a poor farthings-worth of intellect;[A] you are simply a pitiable creature, a behind—your—age disciple of Voltaire. That's what you are."

[Footnote A: Literally, "intellect, in all merely a copeck intellect."]

"Who? I a disciple of Voltaire?"

"Yes, just such a one as your father was; and you have never so much as suspected it."

"After that," exclaimed Lavretsky, "I have a right to say that you are a fanatic."

"Alas!" sorrowfully replied Mikhalevich, "unfortunately, I have not yet in any way deserved so grand a name—"

"I have found out now what to call you!" cried the self-same Mikhalevich at three o'clock in the morning.

"You are not a sceptic, nor are you a *blase*, nor a disciple of Voltaire; you are a marmot,[A] and a culpable marmot; a marmot with a conscience, not a naive marmot. Naive marmots lie on the stove[B] and do nothing, because they can do nothing. They do not even think anything. But you are a thinking man, and yet you lie idly there. You could do something, and you do nothing. You lie on the top with full paunch and say, 'To lie idle—so must it be; because all that people ever do—is all vanity, mere nonsense that conduces to nothing.'"

[Footnote A: A *baibak*, a sort of marmot or "prairie dog."]

[Footnote B: The top of the stove forms the sleeping place in a Russian peasant's hut.]

"But what has shown you that I lie idle?" insisted Lavretsky. "Why do you suppose I have such ideas?"

"—And, besides this, all you people, all your brotherhood," continued Mikhalevich without stopping, "are deeply read marmots. You all know where the German's shoe pinches him; you all know what faults Englishmen and Frenchmen have; and your miserable knowledge only serves to help you to justify your shameful laziness, your abominable idleness. There are some who even pride themselves on this, that 'I, forsooth, am a learned man. I lie idle, and they are fools to give themselves trouble.' Yes! even such persons as these do exist among us; not that I say this with reference to you; such persons as will spend all their life in a certain languor of ennui, and get accustomed to it, and exist in it like—like a mushroom in sour cream" (Mikhalevich could not help laughing at his own comparison). "Oh, that languor of ennui! it is the ruin of the Russian people. Throughout all time the wretched marmot is making up its mind to work—"

"But, after all, what are you scolding about?" cried Lavretsky in his turn. "To work, to do. You had better say what one should do, instead of scolding, O Demosthenes of Poltava."[A]

[Footnote A: Poltava is a town of Little Russia. It will be

remembered that Mikhalovich is a Little Russian.]

"Ah, yes, that's what you want! No, brother, I will not tell you that. Every one must teach himself that," replied Demosthenes in an ironical tone. "A proprietor, a noble, and not know what to do! You have no faith, or you would have known. No faith and no divination."[A]

[Footnote A: *Otkrovenie*, discovery or revelation.]

"At all events, let me draw breath for a moment, you fiend," prayed Lavretsky. "Let me take a look round me!"

"Not a minute's breathing-time, not a second's," replied Mikhalevich, with a commanding gesture of the hand. "Not a single second. Death does not tarry, and life also ought not to tarry."

"And when and where have people taken it into their heads to make marmots of themselves?" he cried at four in the morning, in a voice that was now somewhat hoarse, "Why, here! Why, now! In Russia! When on every separate individual there lies a duty, a great responsibility, before God, before the nation, before himself! We sleep, but time goes by. We sleep—"

"Allow me to point, out to you," observed Lavretsky, "that we do not at all sleep at present, but rather prevent other persons from sleeping. We stretch our throats like barn-door cocks. Listen, that one is crowing for the third time."

This sally made Mikhalevich laugh, and sobered him down. "Good night," he said with a smile, and put away his pipe in its bag. "Good night," said Lavretsky also. However, the friends still went on talking for more than an hour. But their voices did not rise high any longer, and their talk was quiet, sad, kindly talk.

Mikhalevich went away next day, in spite of all his host could do to detain him. Lavretsky did not succeed in persuading him to stay, but he got as much talk as he wanted out of him.

It turned out that Mikhalevich was utterly impecunious. Lavretsky had already been sorry to see in him, on the preceding evening, all the characteristics of a poverty of long standing. His shoes were trodden down, his coat wanted a button behind, his hands were strangers to gloves, one or two bits of feather were sticking in his hair. When he arrived, he did not think of asking for a wash; and at supper he ate like a shark, tearing the meat to pieces with his fingers, and noisily gnawing the bones with his firm, discolored teeth.

It turned out, also, that he had not thriven in the civil service, and that he had pinned all his hopes on the brandy-farmer, who had given him employment simply that he might have an "educated man" in his counting-house. In spite of all this, however, Mikhalevich had not lost courage, but kept on his way leading the life of a cynic, an idealist, and a poet; fervently caring for, and troubling himself about, the destinies of humanity and his special vocation in life—and giving very little heed to the question whether or no he would die of starvation.

Mikhalevich had never married; but he had fallen in love countless times, and he always wrote poetry about all his loves: with especial fervor did he sing about a mysterious, raven-haired "lady." It was rumored, indeed, that this "lady" was nothing more than a Jewess, and one who had numerous friends among cavalry officers; but, after all, if one thinks the matter over, it is not one of much importance.

With Lemm, Mikhalevich did not get on well. His extremely loud way of talking, his rough manners, frightened the German, to whom they were entirely novel. One unfortunate man immediately and from afar recognizes another, but in old age he is seldom willing to associate with him. Nor is that to be wondered at. He has nothing to share with him— not even hopes.

Before he left, Mikhalevich had another long talk with Lavretsky, to whom he predicted utter ruin if he did not rouse himself, and whom he entreated to occupy himself seriously with the question of the position of his serfs. He set himself up as a pattern for imitation, saying that he had been purified in the furnace of misfortune; and then he several times styled himself a happy man, comparing himself to a bird of the air, a lily of the valley.

"A dusky lily, at all events," remarked Lavretsky.

"Ah, brother, don't come the aristocrat," answered Mikhalevich good-humoredly; "but rather thank God that in your veins also there flows simple plebeian blood. But I see you are now in need of some pure, unearthly being, who might rouse you from your apathy."

"Thanks, brother," said Lavretsky; "I have had quite enough of those unearthly beings."

"Silence, cyneec!"[A] exclaimed Mikhalevich.

[Footnote A: He says *Tsuinnik* instead of *Tsinik*.]

"Cynic," said Lavretsky, correcting him.

"Just so, cyneec," repeated the undisconcerted Mikhalevich.

Even when he had taken his seat in the tarantass, in which his flat and marvellously light portmanteau had been stowed away, he still went on talking. Enveloped in a kind of Spanish cloak, with a collar reddened by long use, and with lion's claws instead of hooks, he continued to pour forth his opinions on the destinies of Russia, waving his swarthy hand the while in the air, as if he were sowing the seeds of future prosperity. At last the horses set off.

"Remember my last three words!" he exclaimed, leaning almost entirely out of the carriage, and scarcely able to keep his balance. "Religion, Progress, Humanity! Farewell!" His head, on which his forage cap was pressed down to his eyes, disappeared from sight. Lavretsky was left alone at the door, where he remained gazing attentively along the road, until the carriage was out of sight. "And perhaps he is right," he thought, as he went back into the house. "Perhaps I am a marmot." Much of what Mikhalevich had said had succeeded in winning its way into his heart, although at the time he had contradicted him and disagreed with him. Let a man only be perfectly honest—no one can utterly gainsay him.

XXV

Two days later, Maria Dmitrievna arrived at Vasilievskoe, according to her promise, and all her young people with her. The little girls immediately ran into the garden, but Maria Dmitrievna languidly walked through the house, and languidly praised all she saw. She looked upon her visit to Lavretsky as a mark of great condescension, almost a benevolent action. She smiled affably when Anton and Apraxia came to kiss her hand, according to the old custom of household serfs, and in feeble accents she asked for tea.

To the great vexation of Anton, who had donned a pair of knitted white gloves, it was not he who handed the tea to the lady visitor, but Lavretsky's hired lackey, a fellow who, in the old man's opinion, had not a notion of etiquette. However, Anton had it all his own way at dinner. With firm step, he took up his position behind Madame Kalitine's chair, and he refused to give up his post to any one. The apparition of visitors at Vasilievskoe—a sight for so many years unknown there—both troubled and cheered the old man. It was a pleasure for him to see that his master was acquainted with persons of some standing in society.

Anton was not the only person who was agitated that day. Lemm was excited too. He had put on a shortish snuff-colored coat with pointed tails, and had tied his cravat tight, he coughed incessantly, and made way for every one with kindly and affable mien. As for Lavretsky, he remarked with satisfaction that he remained on the same friendly footing with Liza as before. As soon as she arrived she cordially held out her hand to him.

After dinner, Lemm took a small roll of music-paper out of the tail-pocket of his coat, into which he had been constantly putting his hand, and silently, with compressed lips, placed it upon the piano. It contained a romance, which he had written the day before to some old-fashioned German words, in which mention was made of the stars. Liza immediately sat down to the piano, and interpreted the romance. Unfortunately the music turned out to be confused and unpleasantly constrained. It was evident that the composer had attempted to express some deep and passionate idea, but no result had been attained. The attempt remained an attempt, and nothing more. Both Lavretsky and Liza felt this, and Lemm was conscious of it too. Without saying a word, he put his romance back into his pocket; and, in reply to Liza's proposal to play it over again, he merely shook his head, and said, in a tone of meaning, "For the present—*basta!*" then bent his head, stooped his shoulders, and left the room.

Towards evening they all went out together to fish. In the little lake at the end of the garden there were numbers of carp and groundling. Madame Kalitine had an arm-chair set in the shade for her, near the edge of the water, and a carpet was spread out under her feet. Anton, as an old fisherman of great experience, offered her his services. Zealously did he fasten on the worms, slap them with his hand, and spit upon them, and then fling the line into the water himself, gracefully bending forwards the whole of his body. Maria Dmitrievna had already that day spoken about him to Fedor Ivanovich, using the following phrase of Institute-French:— "*Il n'y a plus maintenant de ces gens comme ca autre fois.*"

Lemm and the two little girls went on to the dam at the end of the lake. Lavretsky placed himself near Liza. The fish kept continually nibbling. Every minute a captured carp glistened in the air with its sometimes golden, sometimes silver, sides. The little girls kept up a ceaseless flow of joyful exclamations. Madame Kalitine herself two or three times uttered a plaintive cry. Lavretsky and Liza caught fewer fish than the others; probably because they paid less attention to their fishing, and let their floats drift up against the edge of the lake. The tall, reddish reeds murmured quietly around them; in front quietly shone the unruffled water, and the conversation they carried on was quiet too.

Liza stood on the little platform [placed there for the use of the washerwomen;] Lavretsky sat on the bent stem of a willow. Liza wore a white dress, fastened round the waist by a broad, white ribbon. From one hand hung her straw hat; with the other she, not without some effort, supported her drooping fishing-rod. Lavretsky gazed at her pure, somewhat severe profile—at the hair turned back behind her ears—at her soft cheeks, the hue of which was like that of a young child's—and thought: "How charming you look, standing there by my lake!" Liza did not look at him, but kept her eyes fixed on the water, something which might be a smile lurking about their corners. Over both Lavretsky and Liza fell the shadow of a neighboring lime-tree.

"Do you know," he began, "I have thought a great deal about our last conversation, and I have come to this conclusion, that you are exceedingly good."

"It certainly was not with that intention that I—" replied Liza, and became greatly confused.

"You are exceedingly good," repeated Lavretsky. "I am a rough-hewn man; but I feel that every one must love you.

There is Lemm, for instance: he's simply in love with you."

Liza's eyebrows did not exactly frown, but they quivered. This always happened with her when she heard anything she did not like.

"I felt very sorry for him to-day, with his unsuccessful romance," continued Lavretsky. "To be young and to want knowledge—that is bearable. But to have grown old and to fail in strength—that is indeed heavy. And the worst of it is, that one doesn't know when one's strength has failed. To an old man such blows are hard to bear. Take care! you've a bite—I hear," continued Lavretsky, after a short pause, "That M. Panshine has written a very charming romance."

"Yes," replied Liza, "it is a small matter; but it isn't bad."

"But what is your opinion about him himself?" asked Lavretsky. "Is he a good musician?"

"I think he has considerable musical faculty. But as yet he has not cultivated it as he ought."

"Just so. But is he a good man?"

Liza laughed aloud, and looked up quickly at Fedor Ivanovich.

"What a strange question!" she exclaimed, withdrawing her line from the water, and then throwing it a long way in again.

"Why strange? I ask you about him as one who has been away from here a long time—as a relation."

"As a relation?"

"Yes. I believe I am a sort of uncle of yours."

"Vladimir Nikolaevich has a good heart," said Liza. "He is clever. Mamma likes him very much."

"But you—do you like him?"

"He is a good man. Why shouldn't I like him?"

"Ah!" said Lavretsky, and became silent. A half-sad, half-mocking expression played upon his face. The fixed look with which he regarded her troubled Liza; but she went on smiling.

"Well, may God grant them happiness!" he murmured at last, as if to himself, and turned away his head.

Liza reddened.

"You are wrong, Fedor Ivanovich," she said; "you are wrong in thinking—But don't you like Vladimir Ivanovich?" she asked suddenly.

"No."

"Why?"

"I think he has no heart."

The smile disappeared from Liza's lips.

"You are accustomed to judge people severely," she said, after a long silence.

"I don't think so. What right have I to judge others severely, I should like to know, when I stand in need of indulgence myself? Or have you forgotten that it is only lazy people who do not mock me? But tell me," he added, "have you kept your promise?"

"What promise?"

"Have you prayed for me?"

"Yes, I prayed for you; and I pray every day. But please do not talk lightly about that."

Lavretsky began to assure Liza that he had never dreamt of doing so—that he profoundly respected all convictions. After that he took to talking about religion, about its significance in the history of humanity, of the meaning of Christianity.

"One must be a Christian," said Liza, not without an effort, "not in order to recognize what is heavenly, or what is earthly, but because every one must die."

With an involuntary movement of surprise, Lavretsky raised his eyes to Liza's, and met her glance.

"What does that phrase of yours mean?" he said.

"It is not my phrase," she replied.

"Not yours? But why did you speak about death?"

"I don't know. I often think about it."

"Often?"

"Yes."

"One wouldn't say so, looking at you now. Your face seems

Ivan S. Turgenev

so happy, so bright, and you smile—"

"Yes. I feel very happy now," replied Liza simply.

Lavretsky felt inclined to seize both her hands and press them warmly.

"Liza, Liza!" cried Madame Kalitine, "come here and see what a carp I have caught."

"Yes, mamma," answered Liza, and went to her.

But Lavretsky remained sitting on his willow stem.

"I talk to her just as if I still had an interest in life," he thought.

Liza had hung up her hat on a bough when she went away. It was with a strange and almost tender feeling that Lavretsky looked at the hat, and at its long, slightly rumpled ribbons.

Liza soon came back again and took up her former position on the platform.

"Why do you think that Vladimir Nikolaevich has no heart?" she asked, a few minutes afterwards.

"I have already told you that I may be mistaken. However, time will reveal all."

Liza became contemplative. Lavretsky began to talk about his mode of life al Vasilievskoe, about Mikhalevich, about Anton. He felt compelled to talk to Liza, to communicate to her all that went on in his heart. And she listened to him so attentively, with such kindly interest; the few remarks and answers she made appeared to him so sensible and so natural. He even told her so.

Liza was astonished. "Really?" she said. "As for me, I thought I was like my maid, Nastasia, and had no words 'of my own.' She said one day to her betrothed, 'You will be sure to be bored with me. You talk to me so beautifully about every thing, but I have no words of my own.'"

"Heaven be praised!" thought Lavretsky.

XXVI

In the meantime the evening had arrived, and Maria Dmitrievna evinced a desire to return home. With some difficulty the little girls were torn away from the lake, and got ready for the journey. Lavretsky said he would accompany his guests half-way home, and ordered a horse to be saddled for him. After seeing Maria Dmitrievna into her carriage he looked about for Lemm; but the old man could nowhere be found. He had disappeared the moment the fishing was over, Anton slammed the carriage door to, with a strength remarkable at his age, and cried in a stern voice, "Drive on, coachman!" The carriage set off. Maria Dmitrievna and Liza occupied the back seats; the two girls and the maid sat in front.

The evening was warm and still, and the windows were open on both sides. Lavretsky rode close by the carriage on Liza's side, resting a hand on the door—he had thrown the reins on the neck of his easily trotting horse—and now and then exchanged two or three words with the young girl. The evening glow disappeared. Night came on, but the air seemed to grow even warmer than before. Maria Dmitrievna soon went to sleep; the little girls and the maid servant slept also. Smoothly and rapidly the carriage rolled on. As Liza bent forwards, the moon, which had only just made its appearance, lighted up her face, the fragrant night air breathed on her eyes and cheeks, and she felt herself happy. Her hand rested on the door of the carriage by the side of Lavretsky's. He too felt himself happy as he floated on in the calm warmth of the night, never moving his eyes away from the good young face, listening to the young voice, clear even in its whispers, which spoke simple, good words.

It even escaped his notice for a time that he had gone more than half of the way. Then he would not disturb Madame Kalitine, but he pressed Liza's hand lightly and said, "We are friends now, are we not?" She nodded assent, and he pulled up his horse. The carriage rolled on its way quietly swinging and curtseying.

Lavretsky returned home at a walk. The magic of the summer night took possession of him. All that spread around him seemed so wonderfully strange, and yet at the same time so well known and so dear. Far and near all was still—and the eye could see very far, though it could not distinguish much of what it saw—but underneath that very stillness a young and flowering life made itself felt.

Lavretsky's horse walked on vigorously, swinging itself steadily to right and left. Its great black shadow moved by its side. There was a sort of secret charm in the tramp of its hoofs, something strange and joyous in the noisy cry of the quails. The stars disappeared in a kind of luminous mist. The moon, not yet at its full, shone with steady lustre. Its light spread in a blue stream over the sky, and fell in a streak of vaporous gold on the thin clouds which went past close at hand.

The freshness of the air called a slight moisture into Lavretsky's eyes, passed caressingly over all his limbs, and flowed with free current into his chest. He was conscious of enjoying, and felt glad of that enjoyment. "Well, we will live on still; she has not entirely deprived us—" he did not say who, or of what.—Then he began to think about Liza; that she could scarcely be in love with Panshine; that if he had met her under other circumstances—God knows what might have come of it; that he understood Lemm's feelings about her now, although she had "no words of her own." And, moreover, that that was not true; for she had words of her own. "Do not speak lightly about that," recurred to Lavretsky's memory. For a long time he rode on with bent head, then he slowly drew himself up repeating,—

"And I have burnt all that I used to worship,
I worship all that I used to burn—"

then he suddenly struck his horse with his whip and and galloped straight away home.

On alighting from his horse he gave a final look round, a thankful smile playing involuntarily on his lips. Night—silent, caressing night—lay on the hills and dales. From its fragrant depths afar—whether from heaven or from earth could not be told—there poured a soft and quiet warmth. Lavretsky wished a last farewell to Liza—and hastened up the steps.

The next day went by rather slowly, rain setting in early in the morning. Lemm looked askance, and compressed his lips even tighter and tighter, as if he had made a vow never to open them again. When Lavretsky lay down at night he took to bed with him a whole bundle of French newspapers, which had already lain unopened on his table for two or three weeks. He began carelessly to tear open their covers and to skim the contents of their columns, in which, for the matter of that, there was but little that was new. He was just on the point of throwing them aside, when he suddenly bounded out of bed as if something had stung him. In the *feuilleton* of one of the papers our former acquaintance, M. Jules, communicated to his readers a "painful piece of intelligence." "The fascinating, fair Muscovite," he wrote, "one of the queens of fashion, the ornament of Parisian salons, Madame de Lavretski," had died almost suddenly. And this news, unfortunately but too true, had just reached him, M. Jules. He was, so he continued, he might say, a friend of the deceased—

Lavretsky put on his clothes, went out into the garden, and walked up and down one of its alleys until the break of day.

At breakfast, next morning, Lemm asked Lavretsky to let him have horses in order to get back to town.

"It is time for me to return to business, that is to lessons," remarked the old man. "I am only wasting my time here uselessly."

Lavretsky did not reply at once. He seemed lost in a reverie.

"Very good," he said at last; "I will go with you myself."

Refusing the assistance of a servant, Lemm packed his little portmanteau, growing peevish the while and groaning over it, and then tore up and burnt some sheets of music paper. The carriage came to the door. As Lavretsky left his study he put in his pocket the copy of the newspaper he had read the night before. During the whole of the journey neither Lavretsky nor Lemm said much. Each of them was absorbed in his own thoughts, and each was glad that the other did not disturb him. And they parted rather coldly, an occurrence which, for the matter of that, often occurs among friends in Russia. Lavretsky drove the old man to his modest dwelling. Lemm took his portmanteau with him as he got out of the carriage, and, without stretching out his hand to his friend, he held the portmanteau before him with both hands, and, without even looking at him, said in Russian, "Farewell!" "Farewell!" echoed Lavretsky, and told the coachman to drive to his apartments; for he had taken lodgings in O.

After writing several letters, and making a hasty dinner, he went to the Kalitines'. There he found no one in the drawing-room but Panshine, who told him that Maria Dmitrievna would come directly, and immediately entered into conversation with him in the kindest and most affable manner. Until that day Panshine had treated Lavretsky, not with haughtiness exactly, but with condescension; but Liza, in describing her excursion of the day before, had spoken of Lavretsky as an excellent and clever man. That was enough; the "excellent" man must be captivated.

Panshine began by complimenting Lavretsky, giving him an account of the rapture with which, according to him, all the Kalitine family had spoken of Vasilievskoe; then, according to his custom, adroitly bringing the conversation round to himself, he began to speak of his occupations, of his views concerning life, the world, and the service; said a word or two about the future of Russia, and about the necessity of holding the Governors of provinces in hand; joked facetiously about himself in that respect, and added that he, among others, had been entrusted at St. Petersburg with the commission *de populariser l'idee du cadastre*. He spoke at tolerable length, and with careless assurance, solving all difficulties, and playing with the most important adminis-trative and political questions as a juggler does with his balls. Such expressions as, "That is what I should do if I were the Government," and, "You, as an intelligent man, doubtless agree with me," were always at the tip of his tongue.

Lavretsky listened coldly to Panshine's eloquence. This handsome, clever, and unnecessarily elegant young man, with his serene smile, his polite voice, and his inquisitive eyes, was not to his liking. Panshine soon guessed, with the quick appreciation of the feelings of others which was peculiar to him, that he did not confer any special gratification on the person he was addressing, so he disappeared under cover of some plausible excuse, having made up his mind that Lavretsky might be an excellent man, but that he was unsympathetic, *"aigri"* and, *en somme*, somewhat ridiculous.

Madame Kalitine arrived, accompanied by Gedeonovsky. Then came Marfa Timofeevna and Liza, and after them all the other members of the family. Afterwards, also, there arrived the lover of music, Madame Belenitsine, a thin little woman, with an almost childish little face, pretty but worn, a noisy black dress, a particolored fan, and thick gold bracelets. With her came her husband, a corpulent man, with red cheeks, large hands and feet, white eyelashes, and a smile which never left his thick lips. His wife never spoke to him in society; and at home, in her tender moments, she used to call him her "sucking pig."

Panshine returned; the room became animated and noisy. Such an assemblage of people was by no means agreeable to Lavretsky. He was especially annoyed by Madame Belenitsine, who kept perpetually staring at him through her eye-glass. If it had not been for Liza he would have gone away at once. He wanted to say a few words to her alone, but for a long time he could not obtain a fitting opportunity of doing so, and had to content himself with following her about with his eyes It was with a secret joy that he did so. Never had her face seemed to him more noble and charming. She appeared to great advantage in the presence of Madame Belenitsine. That lady was incessantly fidgeting on her chair, working her narrow shoulders, laughing affectedly, and either all but closing her eyes or opening them unnaturally

Ivan S. Turgenev

wide. Liza sat still, looked straight before her, and did not laugh at all.

Madame Kalitine sat down to cards with Marfa Timofeevna, Belenitsine, and Gedeonovsky, the latter of whom played very slowly, made continual mistakes, squeezed up his eyes, and mopped his face with his handkerchief. Panshine assumed an air of melancholy, and expressed himself tersely, sadly, and significantly—altogether after the fashion of an artist who has not yet had any opportunity of showing off— but in spite of the entreaties of Madame Belenitsine, who coquetted with him to a great extent he would not consent to sing his romance. Lavretsky's presence embarrassed him.

Lavretsky himself spoke little, but the peculiar expression his face wore struck Liza as soon as he entered the room. She immediately felt that he had something to communicate to her; but, without knowing herself why, she was afraid of asking him any questions. At last, as she was passing into the next room to make the tea, she almost unconsciously looked towards him. He immediately followed her.

"What is the matter with you?" she asked, putting the teapot on the *samovar*.[A]

[Footnote A: Urn.]

"You have remarked something, then?" he said.

"You are different to-day from what I have seen you before."

Lavretsky bent over the table.

"I wanted," he began, "to tell you a piece of news, but just now it is impossible. But read the part of this *feuilleton* which is marked in pencil," he added, giving her the copy of the newspaper he had brought with him. "Please keep the secret; I will come back to-morrow morning."

Liza was thoroughly amazed. At that moment Panshine appeared in the doorway. She put the newspaper in her pocket.

"Have you read Obermann,[A] Lizaveta Mikhailovna?" asked Panshine with a thoughtful air.

[Footnote A: The sentimental romance of that name, written by E. Pivert de Senancour.]

Liza replied vaguely as she passed out of the room, and then went up-stairs. Lavretsky returned into the drawing room and approached the card table. Marfa Timofeevna flushed, and with her cap-strings untied, began to complain to him of her partner Gedeonovsky, who, according to her, had not yet learnt his steps. "Card-playing," she said, "is evidently a very different thing from gossiping." Meanwhile Gedeonovsky never left off blinking and mopping himself with his handkerchief.

Presently Liza returned to the drawing-room and sat down in a corner. Lavretsky looked at her and she at him, and each experienced a painful sensation. He could read perplexity on her face, and a kind of secret reproach. Much as he wished it, he could not get a talk with her, and to remain in the same room with her as a mere visitor among other visitors was irksome to him, so he determined to go away.

When taking leave of her, he contrived to repeat that he would come next day, and he added that he counted on her friendship. "Come," she replied, with the same perplexed look still on her face.

After Lavretsky's departure, Panshine grew animated. He began to give advice to Gedeonovsky, and to make mock love to Madame Belenitsine, and at last he sang his romance. But when gazing at Liza, or talking to her, he maintained the same air as before, one of deep meaning, with a touch of sadness in it.

All that night also, Lavretsky did not sleep. He was not unhappy, he was not agitated; on the contrary, he was perfectly calm; but he could not sleep. He was not even recalling the past. He simply looked at his present life. His heart beat firmly and equably, the hours flew by, he did not even think about sleeping. Only at times there came into his head the thought, "Surely this is not true, this is all nonsense." And then he would stop short, and presently let his head fall back and again betake himself to gazing into the stream of his life.

XXVII

Madame Kalitine did not receive Lavretsky over cordially, when he paid her a visit next day. "Ah! he's making a custom of it," she thought. She was not of herself disposed to like him very much, and Panshine, who had got her thoroughly under his influence, had praised him the evening before in a very astutely disparaging manner. As she did not treat him as an honored guest, nor think it necessary to trouble herself about one who was a relation, almost a member of the family circle, before half an hour had elapsed he went out into the garden. There he and Liza strolled along one of the alleys, while Lenochka and Shurochka played around the flower-pots at a little distance from them.

Liza was as quiet as usual, but more than usually pale. She took the folded leaf of the newspaper from her pocket, and handed it to Lavretsky.

"That is terrible news," she said.

Lavretsky made no reply.

"But, after all, perhaps it may not be true."

"That is why I asked you not to mention it to any one."

Liza walked on a little farther.

"Tell me," she began, "are not you sorry?—not at all sorry?"

"I don't know myself what I feel," answered Lavretsky.

"But you loved her once?"

"I did."

"Very much?"

—"Yes."

"And yet you are not sorry for her death?"

"It is not only now that she has become dead for me."

"You are saying what is sinful. Don't be angry with me. You have called me your friend. A friend may say anything. And it really seems terrible to me. The expression on your face yesterday was not good to see. Do you remember your complaining about her not long ago? And at that very time, perhaps, she was already no longer among the living. It is terrible. It is just as if it had been sent you as a punishment."

Lavretsky laughed bitterly.

"You think so?—at all events I am free now."

Liza shuddered.

"Do not speak so any more. What use is your freedom to you? You should not be thinking of that now, but of forgiveness—"

"I forgave her long ago," interrupted Lavretsky, with an impatient gesture.

"No, I don't mean that," answered Liza, reddening; "you have not understood me properly. It is you who ought to strive to get pardoned."

"Who is there to pardon me?"

"Who? Why God. Who can pardon us except God?"

Lavretsky grasped her hand.

"Ah! Lizaveta Mikhailovna!" he exclaimed, "believe me, I have already been punished enough—I have already expiated all, believe me."

"You cannot tell that," said Liza, in a low voice. "You forget. It was not long ago that you and I were talking, and you were not willing to forgive her."

Both of them walked along the alley for a time in silence.

"And about your daughter?" suddenly asked Liza, and then stopped short.

Lavretsky shuddered.

"Oh! don't disturb yourself about her. I have already sent off letters in all directions. The future of my daughter, as you— as you say—is assured. You need not trouble yourself on that score."

Liza smiled sadly.

"But you are right," continued Lavretsky. "What am I to do

with my freedom—what use is it to me?"

"When did you get this paper?" asked Liza, without answering his question.

"The day after your visit."

"And have not you—have not you even shed a tear?"

"No; I was thunderstruck. But whither should I look for tears? Should I cry over the past? Why, all mine has been, as it were, consumed with fire. Her fault did not actually destroy my happiness; it only proved to me that for me happiness had never really existed. What, then, had I to cry for? Besides—who knows?—perhaps I should have been more grieved if I had received this news a fortnight sooner."

"A fortnight!" replied Liza. "But what can have happened to make such a difference in that fortnight?"

Lavretsky make no reply at first, and Liza suddenly grew still redder than before.

"Yes, yes! you have guessed it!" unexpectedly cried Lavretsky. "In the course of that fortnight I have learnt what a woman's heart is like when it is pure and clear; and my past life seems even farther off from me than it used to be."

Liza became a little uncomfortable, and slowly turned to where Lenochka and Shurochka were in the flower-garden.

"But I am glad I showed you that newspaper," said Lavretsky, as he followed her. "I have grown accustomed to conceal nothing from you, and I hope you will confide in me equally in return."

"Do you really?" said Liza, stopping still. "In that case, I ought. But, no! it is impossible."

"What is it? Tell me—tell me!"

"I really think I ought not.—However," added Liza, turning to Lavretsky with a smile, "what is the good of a half-confidence? Do you know, I received a letter to-day?"

"From Panshine?"

"Yes, from him. How did you guess that?"

"And he asks for your hand?"

"Yes," replied Liza, looking straight at Lavretsky with serious eyes.

Lavretsky, in his turn, looked seriously at Liza.

"Well, and what answer have you made him?" he said at last.

"I don't know what to answer," replied Liza, unfolding her arms, and letting them fall by her side.

"Why? Do you like him?"

"Yes, I like him; I think he is a good man."

"That is just what you told me three days ago, and in the very same words. But what I want to know is, do you love him—love him with that strong, passionate feeling which we usually call 'love'?"

"In the sense in which you understand the word—No."

"You are not in love with him?"

"No. But is that necessary?"

"How do you mean?"

"Mamma likes him," continued Liza. "He is good: I have no fault to find with him."

"But still you waver?"

"Yes—and, perhaps—you, your words are the cause of that. Do you remember what you said the day before yesterday? But all that is weakness—"

"Oh, my child!" suddenly exclaimed Lavretsky, and his voice trembled as he spoke, "don't be fatally wise—don't stigmatize as weakness the cry of your heart, unwilling to give itself away without love! Do not take upon yourself so fearful a responsibility towards that man, whom you do not love, and yet to whom you would be about to belong."

"I shall only be obeying; I shall be taking nothing upon myself," began Liza.

"Obey your own heart, then. It only will tell you the truth," said Lavretsky, interrupting her. "Wisdom, experience—all that is mere vanity and vexation. Do not deprive yourself of the best, the only real happiness upon earth."

"And do you speak in that way. Fedor Ivanovich? You married for love yourself—and were you happy?"

Lavretsky clasped his hands above his head.

"Ah! do not talk about me. You cannot form any idea of

what a young, inexperienced, absurdly brought-up boy may imagine to be love. However, why should one calumniate one's self? I told you just now I had never known happiness. No! I have been happy."

"I think, Fedor Ivanovich," said Liza, lowering her voice— she always lowered her voice when she differed from the person she was speaking to; besides, she felt considerably agitated just then—"our happiness upon earth does not depend upon ourselves—"

"It does depend upon ourselves—upon ourselves:" here he seized both her hands. Liza grew pale and looked at him earnestly, but almost with alarm—"at least if we do not ruin our own lives. For some people a love match may turn out unhappily, but not for you, with your calmness of temperament; with your serenity of soul. I do beseech you not to marry without love, merely from a feeling of duty, self-denial, or the like. All that is sheer infidelity, and moreover a matter of calculation—and worse still. Trust my words. I have a right to say this; a right for which I have paid dearly. And if your God—"

At that moment Lavretsky became aware that Lenochka and Shurochka were standing by Liza's side, and were staring at him with intense astonishment. He dropped Liza's hands, saying hastily, "Forgive me," and walked away towards the house.

"There is only one thing I have to ask you," he said, coming back to Liza. "Don't make up your mind directly, but wait a little, and think over what I have said to you. And even if you don't believe my words, but are determined to marry in accordance with the dictates of mere prudence—even, in that case, Mr. Panshine is not the man you ought to marry. He must not be your husband. You will promise me not to be hasty, won't you?"

Liza wished to reply, but she could not utter a single word. Not that she had decided on being "hasty"—but because her heart beat too strongly, and a feeling resembling that of fear impeded her breathing.

XXVIII

As Lavretsky was leaving the Kalitines' house he met Panshine, with whom he exchanged a cold greeting. Then he went home and shut himself up in his room. The sensations he experienced were such as he had hardly ever known before. Was it long ago that he was in a condition of "peaceful torpor?" Was it long ago that he felt himself, as he had expressed it, "at the very bottom of the river?" What then had changed his condition? What had brought him to the surface, to the light of day? Was the most ordinary and inevitable, though always unexpected, of occurrences—death? Yes. But yet it was not so much his wife's death, his own freedom, that he was thinking about, as this—what answer will Liza give to Panshine?

He felt that in the course of the last three days he had begun to look on Liza with different eyes. He remembered how, when he was returning home and thinking of her in the silence of the night, he said to himself "If!—" This "if," by which at that time he had referred to the past, to the impossible, now applied to an actual state of things, but not exactly such a one as he had then supposed. Freedom by itself was little to him now. "She will obey her mother," he thought. "She will marry Panshine. But even if she refuses him—will it not be just the same as far as I am concerned?" Passing at that moment in front of a looking-glass, he just

Ivan S. Turgenev

glanced at his face in it, and then shrugged his shoulders.

Amid such thoughts as these the day passed swiftly by. The evening arrived, and Lavretsky went to the Kalitines. He walked fast until he drew near to the house, but then he slackened his pace. Panshine's carriage was standing before the door. "Well," thought Lavretsky, as he entered the house, "I will not be selfish." No one met him in-doors, and all seemed quiet in the drawing-room. He opened the door, and found that Madame Kalitine was playing piquet with Panshine. That gentleman bowed to him silently, while the lady of the house exclaimed, "Well, this is an unexpected pleasure," and slightly frowned. Lavretsky sat down beside her and began looking at her cards.

"So you can play piquet?" she asked, with a shade of secret vexation in her voice, and then remarked that she had thrown away a wrong card.

Panshine counted ninety, and began to take up the tricks calmly and politely, his countenance the while wearing a grave and dignified expression. It was thus, he thought, that diplomatists ought to play. It was thus, in all probability, that he used to play with some influential dignitary at St. Petersburg, whom he wished to impress with a favorable idea of his solidity and perspicacity. "One hundred and one, hundred and two, heart, hundred and three," said the measured tones of his voice, and Lavretsky could not tell which it expressed—dislike or assurance.

"Can't I see Marfa Timofeevna?" asked Lavretsky, observing that Panshine, with a still more dignified air than before, was about to shuffle the cards; not even a trace of the artist was visible in him now.

"I suppose so. She is up-stairs in her room," answered Maria

Dmitrievna. "You can ask for her."

Lavretsky went up-stairs. He found Marfa Timofeevna also at cards. She was playing at *Durachki* with Nastasia Carpovna. Roska barked at him, but both the old ladies received him cordially. Marfa Timofeevna seemed in special good humor.

"Ah, Fedia!" she said, "do sit down, there's a good fellow. We shall have done our game directly. Will you have some preserves? Shurochka, give him a pot of strawberries. You won't have any? Well, then, sit there as you are. But as to smoking, you mustn't. I cannot abide your strong tobacco; besides, it would make Matros sneeze."

Lavretsky hastened to assure her that he had not the slightest desire to smoke.

"Have you been down-stairs?" asked the old lady. "Whom did you find there? Is Panshine always hanging about there? But did you see Liza? No? She was to have come here. Why there she is—as soon as one mentions her."

Liza came into the room, caught sight of Lavretsky and blushed.

"I have only come for a moment, Marfa Timofeevna," she was beginning.

"Why for a moment?" asked the old lady. "Why are all you young people so restless? You see I have a visitor there. Chat a little with him, amuse him."

Liza sat down on the edge of a chair, raised her eyes to Lavretsky, and felt at once that she could not do otherwise than let him know how her interview with Panshine had ended. But how was that to be managed? She felt at the same time confused and ashamed. Was it so short a time since she had become acquainted with that man, one who scarcely ever went to church even, and who bore the death of his wife so equably? and yet here she was already communicating her secrets to him. It was true that he took an interest in her; and that, on her side she trusted him, and felt herself drawn towards him. But in spite of all this, she felt a certain kind of modest shame—as if a stranger had entered her pure maiden chamber.

Marfa Timofeevna came to her rescue.

"Well, if you will not amuse him," she said, "who is to amuse him, poor fellow? I am too old for him; he is too clever for me; and as to Nastasia Carpovna, he is too old for her. It's only boys she cares for."

"How can I amuse Fedor Ivanovich?" said Liza. "I would rather play him something on the piano, if he likes," she continued irresolutely.

"That's capital. You're a clever creature," replied Marfa Timofeevna. "Go down-stairs, my dears. Come back again when you've clone; but just now, here I'm left the *durachka*,[A] so I'm savage. I must have my revenge."

[Footnote A: In the game of *durachki*, the player who remains the last is called the *durachok* or *durachka*, diminutive of *durak*, a fool. The game somewhat resembles our own "Old Bachelor" or "Old Maid."]

Liza rose from her chair, and so did Lavretsky. As she was going down-stairs, Liza stopped.

"What they say is true," she began. "The human heart is full of contradictions. Your example ought to have frightened me—ought to have made me distrust marrying for love, and yet I—".

"You've refused him?" said Lavretsky, interrupting her.

"No; but I have not accepted him either. I told him every thing—all my feelings on the subject—and I asked him to wait a little. Are you satisfied?" she asked with a sudden smile: and letting her hand skim lightly along the balustrade, she ran down-stairs.

"What shall I play you?" she asked, as she opened the piano.

"Whatever you like," answered Lavretsky, taking a seat where he could look at her.

Liza began to play, and went on for some time with-out lifting her eyes from her fingers. At last she looked at Lavretsky, and stopped playing. The expression of his face seemed so strange and unusual to her.

"What is the, matter?" she asked.

"Nothing," he replied. "All is well with me at present. I feel happy on your account; it makes me glad to look at you—do go on."

"I think," said Liza, a few minutes later, "if he had really loved me he would not have written that letter; he ought to have felt that I could not answer him just now."

"That doesn't matter," said Lavretsky; "what does matter is that you do not love him."

"Stop! What is that you are saying? The image of your dead

wife is always haunting me, and I feel afraid of you."

"Doesn't my Liza play well, Woldemar?" Madame Kalitine was saying at this moment to Panshine.

"Yes," replied Panshine, "exceedingly well."

Madame Kalitine looked tenderly at her young partner; but he assumed a still more important and pre-occupied look, and called fourteen kings.

XXIX

Lavretsky was no longer a very young man. He could not long delude himself as to the nature of the feeling with which Liza had inspired him. On that day he became finally convinced that he was in love with her. That conviction did not give him much pleasure.

"Is it possible," he thought, "that at five-and-thirty I have nothing else to do than to confide my heart a second time to a woman's keeping? But Liza is not like *her*. She would not have demanded humiliating sacrifices from me. She would not have led me astray from my occupations. She would have inspired me herself with a love for honorable hard work, and we should have gone forward together towards some noble end. Yes," he said, bringing his reflections to a close, "all that is very well. But the worst of it is that she will not go anywhere with me. It was not for nothing that she told me she was afraid of me. And as to her not being in love with Panshine—that is but a poor consolation!"

Lavretsky went to Vasilievskoe; but he could not manage to spend even four days there—so wearisome did it seem to him. Moreover, he was tormented by suspense. The news which M. Jules had communicated required confirmation, and he had not yet received any letters. He returned to town, and passed the evening at the Kalitines'. He could easily see

Ivan S. Turgenev

that Madame Kalitine had been set against him; but he succeeded in mollifying her a little by losing some fifteen roubles to her at piquet. He also contrived to get half-an-hour alone with Liza, in spite of her mother having recommended her, only the evening before, not to be too intimate with a man "*qui a tin si grand ridicule.*"

He found a change in her. She seemed to have become more contemplative. She blamed him for stopping away; and she asked him if he would not go to church the next day—the next day being Sunday.

"Do come," she continued, before he had time to answer. "We will pray together for the repose of *her* soul." Then she added that she did not know what she ought to do—that she did not know whether she had any right to make Panshine wait longer for her decision.

"Why?" asked Lavretsky.

"Because," she replied, "I begin to suspect by this time what that decision will be."

Then she said that she had a headache, and went to her room, after irresolutely holding out the ends of her fingers to Lavretsky.

The next day Lavretsky went to morning service. Liza was already in the church when he entered. He remarked her, though she did not look towards him. She prayed fervently; her eyes shone with a quiet light; quietly she bowed and lifted her head.

He felt that she was praying for him also, and a strange emotion filled his soul. The people standing gravely around, the familiar faces, the harmonious chant, the odor of the incense, the long rays slanting through the windows, the very sombreness of the walls and arches—all appealed to his heart. It was long since he had been in church—long since he had turned his thoughts to God. And even now he did not utter any words of prayer—he did not even pray without words; but nevertheless, for a moment, if not in body, at least in mind, he bowed clown and bent himself humbly to the ground. He remembered how, in the days of his childhood, he always used to pray in church till he felt on his forehead something like a kind of light touch. "That" he used then to think, "is my guardian angel visiting me and pressing on me the seal of election." He looked at Liza. "It is you who have brought me here," he thought. "Touch me—touch my soul!" Meanwhile, she went on quietly praying. Her face seemed to him to be joyous, and once more he felt softened, and he asked, for another's soul, rest—for his own, pardon. They met outside in the porch, and she received him with a friendly look of serious happiness. The sun brightly lit up the fresh grass in the church-yard and the many-colored dresses and kerchiefs of the women. The bells of the neighboring churches sounded on high; the sparrows chirped on the walls. Lavretsky stood by, smiling and bare-headed; a light breeze played with his hair and Liza's, and with the ends of Liza's bonnet strings. He seated Liza and her companion Lenochka, in the carriage, gave away all the change he had about him to the beggars, and then strolled slowly home.

XXX

The days which followed were days of heaviness for Lavretsky. He felt himself in a perpetual fever. Every morning he went to the post, and impatiently tore open his letters and newspapers; but in none of them did he find anything which could confirm or contradict that rumor, on the truth of which he felt that so much now depended. At times he grew disgusted with himself. "What am I," he then would think, "who am waiting here, as a raven waits for blood, for certain intelligence of my wife's death?"

He went to the Kalitines' every day; but even there he was not more at his ease. The mistress of the house was evidently out of humor with him, and treated him with cold condescension. Panshine showed him exaggerated politeness; Lemm had become misanthropical, and scarcely even returned his greeting; and, worst of all, Liza seemed to avoid him. Whenever she happened to be left alone with him, she manifested symptoms of embarrassment, instead of the frank manner of former days. On such occasions she did not know what to say to him; and even he felt confused. In the course of a few days Liza had become changed from what he remembered her to have been. In her movements, in her voice, even in her laugh itself, a secret uneasiness manifested itself—something different from her former evenness of temper. Her mother, like a true egotist, did not suspect anything; but Marfa Timofeevna began to watch her favorite closely.

Lavretsky often blamed himself for having shown Liza the newspaper he had received; he could not help being conscious that there was something in his state of feeling which must be repugnant to a very delicate mind. He supposed, moreover, that the change which had taken place in Liza arose from a struggle with herself, from her doubt as to what answer she should give to Panshine.

One day she returned him a book—one of Walter Scott's novels—which she had herself asked him for.

"Have you read it?" he asked.

"No; I am not in a mood for books just now," she answered, and then was going away.

"Wait a minute," he said. "It is so long since I got a talk with you alone. You seem afraid of me. Is it so?"

"Yes."

"But why?"

"I don't know."

Lavretsky said nothing for a time.

"Tell me," he began again presently; "haven't you made up your mind yet?"

"What do you mean?" she replied, without lifting her eyes from the ground.

"Surely you understand me?"

Liza suddenly reddened.

"Don't ask me about anything!" she exclaimed with animation. "I know nothing. I don't know myself."

And she went hastily away.

The next day Lavretsky arrived at the Kalitines' after dinner, and found all the preparations going on there for an evening service. In a corner of the dining-room, a number of small icons[A] in golden frames, with tarnished little diamonds in the aureolas, were already placed against the wall on a square table, which was covered with a table-cloth of unspotted whiteness. An old servant, dressed in a grey coat and wearing shoes, traversed the whole room deliberately and noiselessly, placed two slender candle-sticks with wax tapers in them before the icons, crossed himself, bowed, and silently left the room.

[Footnote A: Sacred Pictures.]

The drawing-room was dark and empty. Lavretsky went into the dining-room, and asked if it was any one's name-day.[A] He was told in a whisper that it was not, but that a service was to be performed in accordance with the request of Lizaveta Mikhailovna and Marfa Timofeevna. The miracle-working picture was to have been brought, but it had gone to a sick person thirty versts off.

[Footnote A: A Russian keeps, not his birthday, but his name-day—that is, the day set apart by the church in honor of the saint after whom he is called.]

Soon afterwards the priest arrived with his acolytes—a

middle-aged man, with a large bald spot on his head, who coughed loudly in the vestibule. The ladies immediately came out of the boudoir in a row, and asked him for his blessing. Lavretsky bowed to them in silence, and they as silently returned his greeting. The priest remained a little longer where he was, then coughed again, and asked, in a low, deep voice—

"Do you wish me to begin?"

"Begin, reverend father," replied Maria Dmitrievna.

The priest began to robe. An acolyte in a surplice humbly asked for a coal from the fire. The scent of the incense began to spread around. The footmen and the maid-servants came in from the ante-chamber and remained standing in a compact body at the door. The dog Roska, which, as a general rule, never came down-stairs from the upper story, now suddenly made its appearance in the dining room. The servants tried to drive it out, but it got frightened, first ran about, and then lay down. At last a footman got hold of it and carried it off.

The service began. Lavretsky retired into a corner. His feelings were strange and almost painful. He himself could not well define what it was that he felt. Maria Dmitrievna stood in front of the rest, with an arm-chair behind her. She crossed herself carelessly, languidly, like a great lady. Sometimes she looked round, at others she suddenly raised her eyes towards the ceiling. The whole affair evidently bored her.

Marfa Timofeevna seemed pre-occupied. Nastasia Carpovna bowed down to the ground, and raised herself up again, with a sort of soft and modest sound. As for Liza, she did not stir from the spot where she was standing, she did not change her position upon it; from the concentrated expression of her face, it was evident that she was praying uninterruptedly and fervently.

At the end of the service she approached the crucifix, and kissed both it and the large red hand of the priest. Maria Dmitrievna invited him to take tea. He threw off his stole, assumed a sort of mundane air, and went into the drawing-room with the ladies. A conversation began, not of a very lively nature. The priest drank four cups of tea, wiping the bald part of his head the while with his handkerchief, stated among other things that the merchant Avoshnikof had given several hundred roubles towards the gilding of the church's "cumpola," and favored the company with an unfailing cure for freckles.

Lavretsky tried to get a seat near Liza, but she maintained her grave, almost austere air, and never once looked at him. She seemed intentionally to ignore him. A kind of serious, cold enthusiasm appeared to possess her. For some reason or other Lavretsky felt inclined to smile, and to utter words of jesting; but his heart was ill at ease, and at last he went away in a state of secret perplexity. There was something, he felt, in Liza's mind, which he could not understand.

On another occasion, as Lavretsky was sitting in the drawing-room, listening to the insinuating tones of Gedeonovsky's wearisome verbiage, he suddenly turned round, he knew not why, and caught the deep, attentive, inquiring look of Liza's eyes. That enigmatical look was directed towards him. The whole night long Lavretsky thought of it. His love was not like that of a boy, nor was it consistent with his age to sigh and to torment himself; and indeed it was not with a feeling of a merely passionate nature that Liza had inspired him. But love has its sufferings for every age—and he became perfectly acquainted with them.

XXXI

One day Lavretsky was as usual at the Kalitines'. An overpoweringly hot afternoon had been followed by such a beautiful evening that Madame Kalitine, notwithstanding her usual aversion to a draught, ordered all the windows and the doors leading into the garden to be opened. Moreover, she announced that she was not going to play cards, that it would be a sin to do so in such lovely weather, and that it was a duty to enjoy the beauties of nature.

Panshine was the only stranger present. Influenced by the evening, and feeling a flow of artistic emotion, but not wishing to sing in Lavretsky's presence, he threw himself into poetry He read—and read well, only with too much consciousness, and with needlessly subtle distinctions— some of Lermontof's poems (Pushkin had not then succeeded in getting back into fashion). Suddenly, as if ashamed of his emotion, he began in reference to the well-known *Duma*,[A] to blame and attack the new generation, not losing the opportunity which the subject afforded him of setting forth how, if the power lay in his hands, he would alter everything his own way.

[Footnote A: For the poem, so-called, see note at end of chapter.]

Ivan S. Turgenev

"Russia," he said, "has lagged behind Europe, and must be driven up alongside of it. We are told that ours is a young country. That is all nonsense. Besides, we have no inventive power. Khomakof[A] himself admits that we have never invented so much as a mousetrap. Consequently we are obliged to imitate others, whether we like it or no."

[Footnote A: A poet, who was one of the leaders of the Slavophile party.]

"'We are ill,' says Lermontof, and I agree with him. But we are ill because we have only half become Europeans. With that which has wounded us we must be cured." (*"Le cadastre"* thought Lavretsky.) "Among us," he continued, "the best heads, *les meilleures tetes*, have long been convinced of this. In reality, all peoples are alike; only introduce good institutions, and the affair is settled. To be sure, one may make some allowance for the existing life of the nation; that is our business, the business of the people who are" (he all but said "statesmen") "in the public service; but if need arises, don't be uneasy. Those institutions will modify that life itself."

Maria Dmitrievna admiringly agreed with him. "What a clever man to have talking in my house!" she thought. Liza kept silence, leaning back in the recess of the window. Lavretsky kept silence too. Marfa Timofeevna, who was playing cards in a corner with her friend, grumbled something to herself. Panshine walked up and down the room, speaking well, but with a sort of suppressed malice. It seemed as if he was blaming, not so much a whole generation, as some individuals of his acquaintance. A nightingale had made its home in a large lilac bush which stood in the Kalitines' garden, and the first notes of its even-song made themselves heard during the pauses in the eloquent harangue; the first stars began to kindle in the rose-stained sky above the motionless tops of the lime trees. Presently Lavretsky rose and began to reply to Panshine. A warm dispute soon commenced.

Lavretsky spoke in defence of the youth of Russia, and of the capacity of the country to suffice for itself. He surrendered himself and his contemporaries, but he stood up for the new generation, and their wishes and convictions. Panshine replied incisively and irritably, declared that clever people were bound to reform every thing, and at length was carried away to such an extent that, forgetting his position as a chamberlain, and his proper line of action as a member of the civil service, he called Lavretsky a retrogade conservative, and alluded—very distantly it is true—to his false position in society. Lavretsky did not lose his temper, nor did he raise his voice; he remembered that Mikhalevich also had called him a retrograde, and, at the same time a disciple of Voltaire; but he calmly beat Panshine on every point. He proved the impracticability of reforming by sudden bounds, and of introducing changes haughtily schemed on the heights of official self-complacency—changes which were not justified by any intimate acquaintance with the country, nor by a living faith in any ideal, not even in one of negation, and in illustration of this he adduced his own education. He demanded before every thing else that the true spirit of the nation should be recognized, and that it should be looked up to with that humility without which no courage is possible, not even that wherewith to oppose falsehood. Finally he did not attempt to make any defence against what he considered a deserved reproach, that of giving way to a wasteful and inconsiderate expenditure of both time and strength.

"All that is very fine!" at last exclaimed Panshine with vexation. "But here are you, just returned to Russia; what do you intend to do?"

"To cultivate the soil," replied Lavretsky; "and to cultivate it as well as possible."

"No doubt that is very praiseworthy," answered Panshine, "and I hear you have already had great success in that line; but you must admit that every one is not fitted for such an occupation—"

"*Une nature poetique*," said Maria Dmitrievna, "certainly cannot go cultivating the soil—*et puis*, it is your vocation, Vladimir Nikolaevich, to do every thing *en grand*."

This was too much even for Panshine, who grew confused, and changed the conversation. He tried to turn it on the beauty of the starry heavens, on Schubert's music, but somehow his efforts did not prove successful. He ended by offering to play at piquet with Maria Dmitrievna. "What! on such an evening as this?" she feebly objected; but then she ordered the cards to be brought.

Panshine noisily tore open a new pack; and Liza and Lavretsky, as if by mutual consent, both rose from their seats and placed themselves near Marfa Timofeevna. They both suddenly experienced a great feeling of happiness, mingled with a sense of mutual dread, which made them glad of the presence of a third person; at the same time, they both felt that the uneasiness from which they had suffered during the last few days had disappeared, and would return no more.

The old lady stealthily tapped Lavretsky on the cheek, screwed up her eyes with an air of pleasant malice, and shook her head repeatedly, saying in a whisper, "You've done for the genius—thanks!" Then all became still in the room. Nothing was to be heard but the faint crackling of the wax lights, and sometimes the fall of a hand on the table, or an exclamation on the score of points, and the song of the nightingale which, powerful, almost insolently loud, flowed in a great wave through the window, together with the dewy freshness of the night.

*   *   *   *   *

NOTE.—The following is a tolerably literal translation of the poem of Lermontof's to which allusion is made on p. 208, and which created no slight sensation when it first appeared, in the year 1838:—

A THOUGHT.

Sorrowfully do I look upon the present generation! Its future seems either gloomy or meaningless, and meanwhile, whether under the burden of knowledge or of doubt, it grows old in idleness.

When scarcely out of the cradle, we reap the rich inheritance of the errors of our fathers, and the results of their tardy thoughts. Life soon grows wearisome for us, like a banquet at a stranger's festival, like a level road leading nowhere.

In the commencement of our career, we fall away without a struggle, shamefully careless about right and wrong, shamefully timid in the face of danger.

So does a withered fruit which has prematurely ripened— attractive neither to the eye nor to the palate—hang like an alien orphan among blossoms; and the hour of their beauty is that of its fall.

Our intellect has dried up in the pursuit of fruitless science, while we have been concealing the purest of hopes from the knowledge of those who are near and dear to us, and stifling the noble utterance of such sentiments as are ridiculed by a mocking spirit.

We have scarcely tasted of the cup of enjoyment, but for all that we have not husbanded our youthful strength. While we were always in dread of satiety, we have contrived to drain each joy of its best virtues.

No dreams of poetry, no creations of art, touch our hearts with a sweet rapture. We stingily hoard up within our breasts the last remnants of feeling—a treasure concealed by avarice, and which remains utterly unprofitable.

We love and we hate capriciously, sacrificing nothing either to our animosity or to our affection, a certain secret coldness possessing our souls, even while a fire is raging in our veins.

The sumptuous pleasures of our ancestors weary us, as well as their simple, childish diversions. Without enjoying happiness, without reaping glory, we hasten onwards to the grave, casting naught but unlucky glances behind us.

A saturnine crowd, soon to be forgotten, we silently pass away from the world and leave no trace behind, without having handed down to the ages to come a single work of genius, or even a solitary thought laden with meaning.

And our descendants, regarding our memory with the severity of citizens called to sit in judgment on an affair concerning the state, will allude to us with the scathing irony of a ruined son, when he speaks of the father who has squandered away his patrimony.

XXXII

Liza had not uttered a single word during the dispute between Lavretsky and Panshine, but she had followed it attentively, and had been on Lavretsky's side throughout. She cared very little about politics; but she was repelled by the self-sufficient tone of the worldly official, who had never shown himself in that light before, and his contempt for Russia offended her. It had never occurred to Liza to imagine that she was a patriot. But she was thoroughly at her ease with the Russian people. The Russian turn of mind pleased her. She would chat for hours, without thinking anything of it, with the chief of the village on her mother's estate, when he happened to come into town, and talk with him as if he were her equal, without any signs of seigneurial condescension. All this Lavretsky knew well. For his own part, he never would have cared to reply to Panshine; it was only for Liza's sake that he spoke.

They said nothing to each other, and even their eyes but rarely met. But they both felt that they had been drawn closer together that evening, they knew that they both had the same likes and dislikes. On one point only were they at variance; but Liza secretly hoped to bring him back to God. They sat down close by Marfa Timofeevna, and seemed to be following her game; nay, more, did actually follow it. But, meantime, their hearts grew full within them, and nothing

Ivan S. Turgenev

escaped their senses—for them the nightingale sang softly, and the stars burnt, and the trees whispered, steeped in slumberous calm, and lulled to rest by the warmth and softness of the summer night.

Lavretsky gave himself up to its wave of fascination, and his heart rejoiced within him. But no words can express the change that was being worked within the pure soul of the maiden by his side. Even for herself it was a secret; let it remain, then, a secret for all others also. No one knows, no eye has seen or ever will see, how the grain which has been confided to the earth's bosom becomes instinct with vitality, and ripens into stirring, blossoming life.

Ten o'clock struck, and Marfa Timofeevna went up-stairs to her room with Nastasia Carpovna. Lavretsky and Liza walked about the room, stopped in front of the open door leading into the garden, looked first into the gloaming distance and then at each other—and smiled. It seemed as if they would so gladly have taken each other's hands and talked to their hearts' content.

They returned to Maria Dmitrievna and Panshine, whose game dragged itself out to an unusual length. At length the last "king" came to an end, and Madame Kalitine rose from her cushioned chair, sighing, and uttering sounds of weariness the while. Panshine took his hat, kissed her hand, remarked that nothing prevented more fortunate people from enjoying the night or going to sleep, but that he must sit up till morning over stupid papers, bowed coldly to Liza—with whom he was angry, for he had not expected that she would ask him to wait so long for an answer to his proposal—and retired. Lavretsky went away directly after him, following him to the gate, where he took leave of him. Panshine aroused his coachman, poking him in the neck with the end of his stick, seated himself in his droshky, and drove away.

But Lavretsky did not feel inclined to go home, so he walked out of the town into the fields.

The night was still and clear, although there was no moon. For a long time Lavretsky wandered across the dewy grass. A narrow footpath lay in his way, and he followed it. It led him to a long hedge, in which there was a wicket gate. Without knowing why he did so, he tried to push it open; with a faint creak it did open, just as if it had been awaiting the touch of his hand. Lavretsky found himself in a garden, took a few steps along a lime-tree alley, and suddenly stopped short in utter amazement. He saw that he was in the Kalitines' garden.

A thick hazel bush close at hand flung a black patch of shadow on the ground. Into this he quickly passed, and there stood for some time without stirring from the spot, inwardly wondering and from time to time shrugging his shoulders. "This has not happened without some purpose," he thought.

Around all was still. From the house not the slightest sound reached him. He began cautiously to advance. At the corner of an alley all the house suddenly burst upon him with its dusky facade. In two windows only on the upper story were lights glimmering. In Liza's apartment a candle was burning behind the white blind, and in Marfa Timofeevna's bed-room glowed the red flame of the small lamp hanging in front of the sacred picture, on the gilded cover of which it was reflected in steady light. Down below, the door leading on to the balcony gaped wide open.

Lavretsky sat down on a wooden bench, rested his head on his hand, and began looking at that door, and at Liza's window. Midnight sounded in the town; in the house a little clock feebly struck twelve. The watchman beat the hour with quick strokes on his board. Lavretsky thought of nothing, expected nothing. It was pleasant to him to feel himself near Liza, to sit in her garden, and on the bench where she also often sat.

The light disappeared from Liza's room.

"A quiet night to you, dear girl," whispered Lavretsky, still sitting where he was without moving, and not taking his eyes off the darkened window.

Suddenly a light appeared at one of the windows of the lower story, crossed to another window, and then to a third. Some one was carrying a candle through the room. "Can it be Liza? It cannot be," thought Lavretsky. He rose. A well-known face glimmered in the darkness, and Liza appeared in the drawing-room, wearing a white dress, her hair hanging loosely about her shoulders. Quietly approaching the table, she leant over it, put down the candle and began looking for something. Then she turned towards the garden, and crossed to the open door; presently her light, slender, white-robed form stood still on the threshold.

A kind of shiver ran over Lavretsky's limbs, and the word "Liza!" escaped all but inaudibly from his lips.

She started, and then began to peer anxiously into the darkness.

"Liza!" said Lavretsky louder than before, and came out from the shadow of the alley.

Liza was startled. For a moment she bent forward; then she shrank back. She had recognized him. For the third time he called her, and held out his hands towards her. She passed out from the doorway and came into the garden.

"You!" she said. "You here!"

"I—I—Come and hear what I have to say," whispered Lavretsky; and then, taking her hand, he led her to the bench.

She followed him without a word; but her pale face, her fixed look, and all her movements, testified her unutterable astonishment. Lavretsky made her sit down on the bench, and remained standing in front of her.

"I did not think of coming here," he began. "I was led here— I—I—I love you," he ended by saying, feeling very nervous in spite of himself.

Liza slowly looked up at him. It seemed as if it had not been till that moment that she understood where she was, and what was happening to her. She would have risen, but she could not. Then she hid her face in her hands.

"Liza!" exclaimed Lavretsky; "Liza!" he repeated, and knelt down at her feet.

A slight shudder ran over her shoulders; she pressed the fingers of her white hands closer to her face.

"What is it?" said Lavretsky. Then he heard a low sound of sobbing, and his heart sank within him. He understood the meaning of those tears.

"Can it be that you love me?" he whispered, with a caressing gesture of the hand.

"Stand up, stand up, Fedor Ivanovich," she at last succeeded in saying. "What are we doing?"

He rose from his knees, and sat down by her side on the

bench. She was no longer crying, but her eyes, as she looked at him earnestly, were wet with tears.

"I am frightened! What are we doing?" she said again.

"I love you," he repeated. "I am ready to give my whole life for you."

She shuddered again, just as if something had stung her, then she raised her eyes to heaven.

"That is entirely in the hands of God," she replied.

"But you love me, Liza? We are going to be happy?"

She let fall her eyes. He softly drew her to himself, and her head sank upon his shoulder. He bent his head a little aside, and kissed her pale lips.

* * * * *

Half an hour later Lavretsky was again standing before the garden gate. He found it closed now and was obliged to get over the fence. He returned into the town, and walked along its sleeping streets. His heart was full of happiness, intense and unexpected; all misgiving was dead within him. "Disappear, dark spirit of the Past!" he said to himself. "She loves me. She will be mine."

Suddenly he seemed to hear strange triumphal sounds floating in the air above his head. He stopped. With greater grandeur than before the sounds went clanging forth. With strong, sonorous stream did they flow along—and in them, as it seemed to him, all his happiness spoke and sang. He looked round. The sounds came from the two upper windows of a small house.

"Lemm!" he exclaimed, and ran up to the door of the house. "Lemm, Lemm!" he repeated loudly.

The sounds died away, and the form of the old man, wrapped in a dressing-gown, with exposed chest and wildly floating hair, appeared at the window.

"Ha! it is you," he said, with an air of importance.

"Christopher Fedorovich, what wonderful music! For heaven's sake let me in!"

The old man did not say a word, but with a dignified motion of the hand he threw the key of the door out of the window into the street. Lavretsky hastily ran up-stairs, entered the room, and was going to fling himself into Lemm's arms. But Lemm, with a gesture of command, pointed to a chair, and said sharply in his incorrect Russian, "Sit down and listen," then took his seat at the piano, looked round with a proud and severe glance, and began to play.

Lavretsky had heard nothing like it for a long time indeed. A sweet, passionate melody spoke to the heart with its very first notes. It seemed all thoroughly replete with sparkling light, fraught with inspiration, with beauty, and with joy. As it rose and sank it seemed to speak of all that is dear, and secret, and holy, on earth. It spoke too of a sorrow that can never end, and then it went to die away in the distant heaven.

Lavretsky had risen from his seat and remained standing, rooted to the spot, and pale with rapture. Those sounds entered very readily into his heart; for it had just been stirred into sensitiveness by the touch of a happy love, and they themselves were glowing with love.

"Play it again," he whispered, as soon as the last final chord had died away.

The old man looked at him with an eagle's glance, and said slowly, in his native tongue, striking his breast with his hand, "It is I who wrote that, for I am a great musician," and then he played once more his wonderful composition.

There were no lights in the room, but the rays of the rising moon entered obliquely through the window. The listening air seemed to tremble into music, and the poor little apartment looked like a sanctuary, while the silvery half-light gave to the head of the old man a noble and spiritual expression.

Lavretsky came up to him and embraced him. At first Lemm did not respond to his embrace—even put him aside with his elbow. Then he remained rigid for some time, without moving any of his limbs, wearing the same severe, almost repellent, look as before, and only growling out twice, "Aha!" But at last a change came over him, his face grew calm, and his head was no longer thrown back. Then, in reply to Lavretsky's warm congratulations, he first smiled a little, and afterwards began to cry, sobbing faintly, like a child.

"It is wonderful," he said, "your coming just at this very moment. But I know every thing—I know all about it."

"You know every thing?" exclaimed Lavretsky in astonishment.

"You have heard what I said," replied Lemm. "Didn't you understand that I knew every thing?"

* * * * *

Lavretsky did not get to sleep till the morning. All night long he remained sitting on the bed. Neither did Liza sleep. She was praying.

Ivan S. Turgenev

XXXIII

The reader knows how Lavretsky had been brought up and educated. We will now say a few words about Liza's education. She was ten years old when her father died, who had troubled himself but little about her. Overwhelmed with business, constantly absorbed in the pursuit of adding to his income, a man of bilious temperament and a sour and impatient nature, he never grudged paying for the teachers and tutors, or for the dress and the other necessaries required by his children, but he could not bear "to nurse his squallers," according to his own expression—and, indeed, he never had any time for nursing them. He used to work, become absorbed in business, sleep a little, play cards on rare occasions, then work again. He often compared himself to a horse yoked to a threshing machine. "My life has soon been spent," he said on his death-bed, a bitter smile contracting his lips.

As to Maria Dmitrievna, she really troubled herself about Liza very little more than her husband did, for all that she had taken credit to herself, when speaking to Lavretsky, for having educated her children herself. She used to dress her like a doll, and when visitors were present, she would caress her and call her a good child and her darling, and that was all. Every continuous care troubled that indolent lady.

During her father's lifetime, Liza was left in the hands of a governess, a Mademoiselle Moreau, from Paris; but after his death she passed under the care of Marfa Timofeevna. That lady is already known to the reader. As for Mademoiselle Moreau, she was a very small woman, much wrinkled, and having the manners of a bird, and the character of a bird also. In her youth she had led a very dissipated life; in her old age she retained only two passions—the love of dainties and the love of cards. When her appetite was satiated, and when she was not playing cards or talking nonsense, her countenance rapidly assumed an almost death-like expression. She would sit and gaze and breathe, but it was plain that there was not a single idea stirring in her mind. She could not even be called good; goodness is not an attribute of birds. In consequence either of her frivolous youth or of the air of Paris, which she had breathed from her childhood's days, there was rooted in her a kind of universal scepticism, which usually found expression in the words, "*Tout ca c'est des betises.*" She spoke an incorrect, but purely Parisian jargon, did not talk scandal, and had no caprices—what more could one expect from a governess? Over Liza she had but little influence. All the more powerful, then, was the influence exercised over the child by her nurse, Agafia Vlasievna.

That woman's story was a remarkable one. She sprang from a family of peasants, and was married at sixteen to a peasant; but she stood out in sharp relief against the mass of her peasant sisters. As a child, she had been spoilt by her father, who had been for twenty years the head of his commune, and who had made a good deal of money. She was singularly beautiful, and for grace and taste she was unsurpassed in the whole district, and she was intelligent, eloquent, and courageous. Her master, Dmitry Pestof, Madame Kalitine's father, a quiet and reserved man, saw her one day on the threshing-floor, had a talk with her, and fell passionately in love with her. Soon after this she became a widow. Pestof,

Ivan S. Turgenev

although he was a married man, took her into his house, and had her dressed like one of the household. Agafia immediately made herself at home in her new position, just as if she had never led a different kind of life. Her complexion grew fairer, her figure became more rounded, and her arms, under their muslin sleeves, showed "white as wheat-flour," like those of a wealthy tradesman's wife. The *samovar* never quitted her table; she would wear nothing but silks and velvets; she slept on feather-beds of down.

This happy life lasted five years; then Dmitry Pestof died. His widow, a lady of a kindly character, respected the memory of her late husband too much to wish to treat her rival with ignominy, especially as Agafia had never forgotten herself in her presence; but she married her to a herdsman, and sent her away from her sight. Three years passed by. One hot summer day the lady happened to pay a visit to the cattle-yard. Agafia treated her to such a cool dish of rich cream, behaved herself so modestly, and looked so clean, so happy, so contented with every thing, that her mistress informed her that she was pardoned, and allowed her to return into the house. Before six months had passed, the lady had become, so attached to her that she promoted her to the post of housekeeper, and confided all the domestic arrangements to her care. Thus Agafia came back into power, and again became fair and plump. Her mistress trusted her implicitly.

So passed five more years. Then misfortune came a second time on Agafia. Her husband, for whom she had obtained a place as footman, took to drink, began to absent himself from the house, and ended by stealing half-a-dozen of his mistress's silver spoons and hiding them, till a fitting opportunity should arise for carrying them off in his wife's box. The theft was found out. He was turned into a herdsman again, and Agafia fell into disgrace. She was not dismissed from the house, but she was degraded from the position of housekeeper to that of a needle-woman, and she was ordered to wear a handkerchief on her head instead of a cap. To every one's astonishment, Agafia bore the punishment inflicted on her with calm humility. By this time she was about thirty years old, all her children were dead, and her husband soon afterwards died also. The season of reflection had arrived for her, and she did reflect. She became very silent and very devout, never once letting matins or mass go unheeded by, and she gave away all her fine clothes. For fifteen years she led a quiet, grave, peaceful life, quarrelling with no one, giving way to all. If any one spoke to her harshly, she only bent her head and returned thanks for the lesson. Her mistress had forgiven her long ago, and had taken the ban off her—had even given her a cap off her own head to wear. But she herself refused to doff her handkerchief, and she would never consent to wear any but a sombre-colored dress. After the death of her mistress she became even more quiet and more humble than before. It is easy to work upon a Russian's fears and to secure his attachment, but it is difficult to acquire his esteem; that he will not readily give, nor will he give it to every one. But the whole household esteemed Agafia. No one even so much as remembered her former faults; it was as if they had been buried in the grave with her old master.

When Kalitine married Maria Dmitrievna, he wanted to entrust the care of his household to Agafia; but she refused, "on account of temptation." He began to scold her, but she only bowed low and left the room. The shrewd Kalitine generally understood people; so he understood Agafia's character, and did not lose sight of her. When he settled in town, he appointed her, with her consent, to the post of nurse to Liza, who was then just beginning her fifth year.

At first Liza was frightened by the serious, even severe, face of her new nurse; but she soon became accustomed to her, and learned to love her warmly. The child was of a serious disposition herself. Her features called to mind Kalitine's regular and finely-moulded face, but her eyes were not like those of her father; they shone with a quiet light, expressive of an earnest goodness that is rarely seen in children. She did not care about playing with dolls; she never laughed loudly nor long, and a feeling of self-respect always manifested itself in her conduct. It was not often that she fell into a reverie, but when she did so there was almost always good reason for it; then she would keep silence for a time, but generally ended by addressing to some person older than herself a question which showed that her mind had been working under the influence of a new impression. She very soon got over her childish lisp, and even before she was four years old she spoke with perfect distinctness. She was afraid of her father. As for her mother, she regarded her with a feeling which she could scarcely define, not being afraid of her, but not behaving towards her caressingly. As for that, she did not caress even her nurse, although she loved her with her whole heart. She and Agafia were never apart. It was curious to see them together. Agafia, all in black, with a dark handkerchief on her head, her face emaciated and of a wax-like transparency, but still beautiful and expressive, would sit erect on her chair, knitting stockings. At her feet Liza would be sitting on a little stool, also engaged in some work, or, her clear eyes uplifted with a serious expression, listening to what Agafia was telling her. Agafia never told her nursery tales. With a calm and even voice, she used to tell her about the life of the Blessed Virgin, or the lives of the hermits and people pleasing to God, or about the holy female martyrs. She would tell Liza how the saints lived in the deserts; how they worked out their salvation, enduring hunger and thirst; and how they did not fear kings, but confessed Christ; and how the birds of the air brought them food, and the wild beasts obeyed them; how from those spots where their blood had fallen flowers sprang up. ("Were they carnations?" once asked Liza, who was very fond of flowers.) Agafia spoke about these things to Liza seriously and humbly, as if she felt that it was not for her to pronounce such grand and holy words; and as Liza listened to her, the image of the Omnipresent, Omniscient God entered with a sweet influence into her very soul, filling her with a pure and reverend dread, and Christ seemed to her to be close to her, and to be a friend, almost, as it were, a relation. It was Agafia, also, who taught her to pray. Sometimes she awoke Liza at the early dawn, dressed her hastily, and secretly conveyed her to matins. Liza would follow her on tiptoe, scarcely venturing to breathe. The cold, dim morning light, the raw air pervading the almost empty church, the very secrecy of those unexpected excursions, the cautious return home to bed—all that combination of the forbidden, the strange, the holy, thrilled the young girl, penetrated to the inmost depths of her being.

Agafia never blamed any one, and she never scolded Liza for any childish faults. When she was dissatisfied about anything, she merely kept silence, and Liza always understood that silence. With a child's quick instinct, she also knew well when Agafia was dissatisfied with others, whether it were with Maria Dmitrievna or with Kalitine himself.

For rather more than three years Agafia waited upon Liza. She was replaced by Mademoiselle Moreau; but the frivolous Frenchwoman, with her dry manner and her constant exclamation, *Tout ca c'est des betises!* could not expel from Liza's heart the recollection of her much-loved nurse. The seeds that had been sown had pushed their roots too far for that. After that Agafia, although she had ceased to attend Liza, remained for some time longer in the house, and often saw her pupil, and treated her as she had been used to do.

But when Marfa Timofeevna entered the Kalitines' house, Agafia did not get on well with her. The austere earnestness of the former "wearer of the coarse petticoat." [Footnote: The *Panovnitsa*, or wearer of the *Panovna*, a sort of petticoat made of a coarse stuff of motley hue.] did not please the impatient and self-willed old lady. Agafia obtained leave to go on a pilgrimage, and she never came back. Vague rumors asserted that she had retired into a schismatic convent. But the impression left by her on Liza's heart did not disappear. Just as before, the girl went to mass, as if she were going to a festival; and when in church prayed with enthusiasm, with a kind of restrained and timid rapture, at which her mother secretly wondered not a little. Even Marfa Timofeevna, although she never put any constraint upon Liza, tried to induce her to moderate her zeal, and would not let her make so many prostrations. It was not a lady-like habit, she said.

Liza was a good scholar, that is, a persevering one; she was not gifted with a profound intellect, or with extraordinarily brilliant faculties, and nothing yielded to her without demanding from her no little exertion. She was a good pianiste, but no one else, except Lemm, knew how much that accomplishment had cost her. She did not read much, and she had no "words of her own;" but she had ideas of her own, and she went her own way. In this matter, as well as in personal appearance, she may have taken after her father, for he never used to ask any one's advice as to what he should do.

And so she grew up, and So did her life pass, gently and tranquilly, until she had attained her nineteenth year. She was very charming, but she was not conscious of the fact. In all her movements, a natural, somewhat unconventional, grace, revealed itself; in her voice there sounded the silver notes of early youth. The slightest pleasurable sensation would bring a fascinating smile to her lips, and add a deeper light, a kind of secret tenderness, to her already lustrous eyes. Kind and soft-hearted, thoroughly penetrated by a feeling of duty, and a fear of injuring any one in any way, she was attached to all whom she knew, but to no one person in particular. To God alone did she consecrate her love— loving Him with a timid, tender enthusiasm. Until Lavretsky came, no one had troubled the calmness of her inner life.

Such was Liza.

XXXIV

About the middle of the next day Lavretsky went to the Kalitines'. On his way there he met Panshine, who galloped past on horseback, his hat pulled low over his eyes. At the Kalitines', Lavretsky was not admitted, for the first time since he had made acquaintance with the family. Maria Dmitrievna was asleep, the footman declared; her head ached, Marfa Timofeevna and Lizaveta Mikhailovna were not at home.

Lavretsky walked round the outside of the garden in the vague hope of meeting Liza, but he saw no one. Two hours later he returned to the house, but received the same answer as before; moreover, the footman looked at him in a somewhat marked manner. Lavretsky thought it would be unbecoming to call three times in one day, so he determined to drive out to Vasilievskoe, where, moreover, he had business to transact.

On his way there he framed various plans, each one more charming than the rest. But on his arrival at his aunt's estate, sadness took hold of him. He entered into conversation with Anton; but the old man, as if purposely, would dwell on none but gloomy ideas. He told Lavretsky how Glafira Petrovna, just before her death, had bitten her own hand. And then, after an interval of silence, he added with a sigh, "Every man, *barin batyushka*,[A] is destined to devour himself."

[Footnote A: Seigneur, father.]

It was late in the day before Lavretsky set out on his return. The music he had heard the night before came back into his mind, and the image of Liza dawned on his heart in all its sweet serenity. He was touched by the thought that she loved him; and he arrived at his little house in the town, tranquillized and happy.

The first thing that struck him when he entered the vestibule, was a smell of patchouli, a perfume he disliked exceedingly. He observed that a number of large trunks and boxes were standing there, and he thought there was a strange expression on the face of the servant who hastily came to meet him. He did not stop to analyze his impressions, but went straight into the drawing-room.

A lady, who wore a black silk dress with flounces, and whose pale face was half hidden by a cambric handkerchief, rose from the sofa, took a few steps to meet him, bent her carefully-arranged and perfumed locks—and fell at his feet. Then for the first time, he recognized her. That lady was his wife!

His breathing stopped. He leaned against the wall.

"Do not drive me from you, Theodore!" she said in French; and her voice cut him to the heart like a knife. He looked at her without comprehending what he saw, and yet, at the same time, he involuntarily remarked that she had grown paler and stouter.

"Theodore!" she continued, lifting her eyes from time to time towards heaven, her exceedingly pretty fingers, tipped with polished nails of rosy hue, writhing the while in preconcerted agonies—"Theodore, I am guilty before you—deeply guilty. I will say more—I am a criminal; but hear what I have to say. I am tortured by remorse; I have become a burden to myself; I can bear my position no longer. Ever so many times I have thought of addressing you, but I was afraid of your anger. But I have determined to break every tie with the past—*puis, j'ai ete si malade*. I was so ill," she added, passing her hand across her brow and cheek, "I took advantage of the report which was spread abroad of my death, and I left everything. Without stopping anywhere, I travelled day and night to come here quickly. For a long time I was in doubt whether to appear before you, my judge—*paraitre devant vous man juge*; but at last I determined to go to you, remembering your constant goodness. I found out your address in Moscow. Believe me," she continued, quietly rising from the ground and seating herself upon the very edge of an arm-chair, "I often thought of death, and I could have found sufficient courage in my heart to deprive myself of life—ah! life is an intolerable burden to me now—but the thought of my child, my little Ada, prevented me. She is here now; she is asleep in the next room, poor child. She is tired out You will see her, won't you? She, at all events, is innocent before you; and so unfortunate—so unfortunate!" exclaimed Madame Lavretsky, and melted into tears.

Lavretsky regained his consciousness at last. He stood away from the wall, and turned towards the door.

"You are going away?" exclaimed his wife, in accents of despair. "Oh, that is cruel! without saying a single word to me—not even one of reproach! This contempt kills me; it is dreadful!"

Lavretsky stopped.

"What do you want me to say to you?" he said in a hollow tone.

"Nothing—nothing!" she cried with animation. "I know that I have no right to demand anything. I am no fool, believe me. I don't hope, I don't dare to hope, for pardon. I only venture to entreat you to tell me what I ought to do, where I ought to live. I will obey your orders like a slave, whatever they may be."

"I have no orders to give," replied Lavretsky in the same tone as before. "You know that all is over between us—and more than ever now. You can live where you like; and if your allowance is too small—"

"Ah, don't say such terrible things!" she said, interrupting him. "Forgive me, if only—if only for the sake of this angel."

And having uttered these words, Varvara Pavlovna suddenly rushed into the other room, and immediately returned with a very tastefully-dressed little girl in her arms. Thick flaxen curls fell about the pretty little rosy face and over the great black, sleepy eyes of the child, who smilingly blinked at the light, and held on to her mother's neck by a chubby little arm.

"*Ada, vois, c'est ton pere,*" said Varvara Pavlovna, removing the curls from the child's eyes, and kissing her demonstratively. "*Prie-le avec moi.*"

"*C'est la, papa?*" the little girl lispingly began to stammer.

"*Oui, mon enfant, n'est-ce pas que tu l'aimes?*"

But the interview had become intolerable to Lavretsky.

"What melodrama is it just such a scene occurs; in?" he

muttered, and left the room.

Varvara Pavlovna remained standing where she was for some time, then she slightly shrugged her shoulders, took the little girl back into the other room, undressed her, and put her to bed. Then she took a book and sat down near the lamp. There she waited about an hour, but at last she went to bed herself.

"*Eh bien, madame*?" asked her maid,—a Frenchwoman whom she had brought with her from Paris,—as she unlaced her stays.

"*Eh bien*, Justine!" replied Varvara Pavlovna. "He has aged a great deal, but I think he is just as good as ever. Give me my gloves for the night, and get the gray dress, the high one, ready for to-morrow morning—and don't forget the mutton cutlets for Ada. To be sure it will be difficult to get them here, but we must try."

"*A la guerre comme a la guerre*!" replied Justine as she put out the light.

XXXV

For more than two hours Lavretsky wandered about the streets. The night he had spent in the suburbs of Paris came back into his mind. His heart seemed rent within him, and his brain felt vacant and as it were numbed, while the same set of evil, gloomy, mad thoughts went ever circling in his mind. "She is alive; she is here," he whispered to himself with constantly recurring amazement. He felt that he had lost Liza. Wrath seemed to suffocate him. The blow had too suddenly descended upon him. How could he have so readily believed the foolish gossip of a *feuilleton*, a mere scrap of paper? "But if I had not believed it," he thought, "what would have been the difference? I should not have known that Liza loves me. She would not have known it herself." He could not drive the thought of his wife out of his mind; her form, her voice, her eyes haunted him. He cursed himself, he cursed every thing in the world.

Utterly tired out, he came to Lemm's house before the dawn. For a long time he could not get the door opened; at last the old man's nightcapped head appeared at the window. Peevish and wrinkled, his face bore scarcely any resemblance to that which, austerely inspired, had looked royally down upon Lavretsky twenty-four hours before, from all the height of its artistic grandeur.

Ivan S. Turgenev

"What do you want?" asked Lemm. "I cannot play every night. I have taken a *tisane*."

But Lavretsky's face wore a strong expression which could not escape notice. The old man shaded his eyes with his hand, looked hard at his nocturnal visitor, and let him in.

Lavretsky came into the room and dropped on a chair. The old man remained standing before him, wrapping the skirts of his motley old dressing-gown around him, stooping very much, and biting his lips.

"My wife has come," said Lavretsky, with drooping head, and then he suddenly burst into a fit of involuntary laughter.

Lemm's face expressed astonishment, but he preserved a grave silence, only wrapping his dressing-gown tighter around him.

"I suppose you don't know," continued Lavretsky. "I supposed—I saw in a newspaper that she was dead."

"O—h! Was it lately you saw that?" asked Lemm.

"Yes."

"O—h!" repeated the old man, raising his eyebrows, "and she has come here?"

"Yes. She is now in my house, and I—I am a most unfortunate man."

And he laughed again.

"You are a most unfortunate man," slowly repeated Lemm.

"Christopher Fedorovich," presently said Lavretsky, "will you undertake to deliver a note?"

"Hm! To whom, may I ask?"

"To Lizav—"

"Ah! yes, yes, I understand. Very well. But when must the note be delivered?"

"To-morrow, as early as possible."

"Hm! I might send my cook, Katrin. No, I will go myself."

"And will you bring me back the answer?"

"I will."

Lemm sighed.

"Yes, my poor young friend," he said, "you certainly are—a most unfortunate young man."

Lavretsky wrote a few words to Liza, telling her of his wife's arrival, and begging her to make an appointment for an interview. Then he flung himself on the narrow sofa, with his face to the wall. The old man also lay down on his bed, and there long tossed about, coughing and swallowing mouthfuls of his *tisane*.

The morning came; they both arose—strange were the looks they exchanged. Lavretsky would have liked to kill himself just then. Katrin the cook brought them some bad coffee, and then, when eight o'clock struck, Lemm put on his hat and went out saying that he was to have given a lesson at the Kalitines' at ten o'clock, but that he would find a fitting excuse for going there sooner.

Lavretsky again threw himself on the couch, and again a bitter laugh broke out from the depths of his heart. He thought of how his wife had driven him out of the house; he pictured to himself Liza's position, and then he shut his eyes, and wrung his hands above his head.

At length Lemm returned and brought him a scrap of paper, on which Liza had traced the following words in pencil: "We cannot see each other to-day; perhaps we may to-morrow evening. Farewell." Lavretsky thanked Lemm absently and stiffly, and then went home.

He found his wife at breakfast. Ada, with her hair all in curl-papers, and dressed in a short white frock with blue ribbons, was eating a mutton cutlet. Varvara Pavlovna rose from her seat the moment Lavretsky entered the room, and came towards him with an expression of humility on her face. He asked her to follow him into his study, and when there he shut the door and began to walk up and down the room. She sat down, folded her hands, and began to follow his movements with eyes which were still naturally beautiful, besides having their lids dyed a little.

For a long time Lavretsky could not begin what he had to say, feeling that he had not complete mastery over himself. As for his wife, he saw that she was not at all afraid of him, although she looked as if she might at any moment go off into a fainting fit.

"Listen, Madame," at last he began, breathing with difficulty, and at times setting his teeth hard. "There is no reason why we should be hypocritical towards each other. I do not believe in your repentance; but even if it were genuine, it would be impossible for me to rejoin you and live with you again."

Varvara Pavlovna bit her lips and half closed her eyes. "That's dislike," she thought. "It's all over. I'm not even a woman for him."

"Impossible," repeated Lavretsky, and buttoned his coat. "I don't know why you have been pleased to honor me by coming here. Most probably you are out of funds."

"Don't say that—you wound my feelings," whispered Varvara Pavlovna.

"However that may be, you are still, to my sorrow, my wife. I cannot drive you away, so this is what I propose. You can go to Lavriki—to-day if you like—and live there! There is an excellent house there, as you know. You shall have every thing you can want, besides your allowance. Do you consent?"

Varvara Pavlovna raised her embroidered handkerchief to her face.

"I have already told you," she said, with a nervous twitching of her lips, "that I will agree to any arrangement you may please to make for me. At present I have only to ask you— will you at least allow me to thank you for your generosity?"

"No thanks, I beg of you—we shall do much better without them," hastily exclaimed Lavretsky. "Then, he added, approaching the door, I may depend upon—"

"To-morrow I will be at Lavriki," replied Varvara Pavlovna, rising respectfully from her seat. "But Fedor Ivanich—" ("She no longer familiarly called him Theodore).

"What do you wish to say?"

"I am aware that I have not yet in any way deserved forgiveness. But may I hope that, at least, in time—"

"Ah, Varvara Pavlovna," cried Lavretsky, interrupting her, "you are a clever woman; but I, too, am not a fool. I know well that you have no need of forgiveness. Besides, I forgave you long ago; but there has always been a gulf between you and me."

"I shall know how to submit," answered Varvara Pavlovna, and bowed her head. "I have not forgotten my fault. I should not have wondered if I had learnt that you had even been glad to hear of my death," she added in a soft voice, with a slight wave of her hand towards the newspaper, which was lying on the table where Lavretsky had forgotten it.

Lavretsky shuddered. The *feuilleton* had a pencil mark against it. Varvara Pavlovna gazed at him with an expression of even greater humility than before on her face. She looked very handsome at that moment. Her grey dress, made by a Parisian milliner, fitted closely to her pliant figure, which seemed almost like that of a girl of seventeen. Her soft and slender neck, circled by a white collar, her bosom's gentle movement under the influence of her steady breathing, her arms and hands, on which she wore neither bracelets nor rings, her whole figure, from her lustrous hair to the tip of the scarcely visible *bottine*, all was so artistic!

Lavretsky eyed her with a look of hate, feeling hardly able to abstain from crying *brava*, hardly able to abstain from striking her down—and went away.

An hour later he was already on the road to Vasilievskoe, and two hours later Varvara Pavlovna ordered the best carriage on hire in the town to be got for her, put on a simple straw hat with a black veil, and a modest mantilla, left Justine in charge of Ada, and went to the Kalitines'. From the inquiries Justine had made, Madame Lavretsky had learnt that her husband was in the habit of going there every day.

XXXVI

The day on which Lavretsky's wife arrived in O.—sad day for him—was also a day of trial for Liza. Before she had had time to go down-stairs and say good morning to her mother, the sound of a horse's hoofs was heard underneath the window, and, with a secret feeling of alarm, she saw Panshine ride into the court-yard. "It is to get a definite answer that he has come so early," she thought; and she was not deceived. After taking a turn through the drawing-room, he proposed to go into the garden with her; and when there he asked her how his fate was to be decided.

Liza summoned up her courage, and told him that she could not be his wife. He listened to all she had to say, turning himself a little aside, with his hat pressed down over his eyes. Then, with perfect politeness, but in an altered tone, he asked her if that was her final decision, and whether he had not, in some way or other, been the cause of such a change in her ideas. Then he covered his eyes with his hand for a moment, breathed one quick sigh, and took his hand away from his face.

"I wanted to follow the beaten track," he said sadly; "I wanted to choose a companion for myself according to the dictates of my heart. But I see that it is not to be. So farewell to my fancy!"

He made Liza a low bow, and went back into the house.

She hoped he would go away directly; but he went to her mother's boudoir, and remained an hour with her. As he was leaving the house he said to Liza, "*Votre mere vous appelle: Adieu a jamais*!" then he got on his horse, and immediately set off at full gallop.

On going to her mother's room, Liza found her in tears. Panshine had told her about his failure.

"Why should you kill me? Why should you kill me?" Thus did the mortified widow begin her complaint. "What better man do you want? Why is he not fit to be your husband? A chamberlain! and so disinterested Why, at Petersburg he might marry any of the maids of honor! And I—I had so longed for it. And how long is it since you changed your mind about him? Wherever has this cloud blown from?—for it has never come of its own accord. Surely it isn't that wiseacre? A pretty adviser you have found, if that's the case!"

"And as for him, my poor, dear friend," continued Maria Dmitrievna, "how respectful he was, how attentive, even in the midst of his sorrow! He has promised not to desert me. Oh, I shall never be able to bear this! Oh, my head is beginning to ache dreadfully! Send Palashka here. You will kill me, if you don't think better of it. Do you hear?" And then, after having told Liza two or three times that she was ungrateful, Maria Dmitrievna let her go away.

Liza went to her room. But before she had had a moment's breathing-time after her scene with Panshine and with her mother, another storm burst upon her, and that from the quarter from which she least expected it.

Marfa Timofeevna suddenly came into her room, and immediately shut the door after her. The old lady's face was pale; her cap was all awry; her eyes were flashing, her lips quivering. Liza was lost in astonishment. She had never seen her shrewd and steady aunt in such a state before.

"Very good, young lady!" Marfa Timofeevna began to whisper, with a broken and trembling voice. "Very good! Only who taught that, my mother—Give me some water; I can't speak."

"Do be calm, aunt. What is the matter?" said Liza, giving her a glass of water. "Why, I thought you didn't like M. Panshine yourself."

Marfa Timofeevna pushed the glass away. "I can't drink it. I should knock out my last teeth, if I tried. What has Panshine to do with it? Whatever have we to do with Panshine? Much better tell me who taught you to make appointments with people at night. Eh, my mother!"

Liza turned very pale.

"Don't try to deny it, please," continued Marfa Timofeevna. "Shurochka saw it all herself, and told me. I've had to forbid her chattering, but she never tells lies."

"I am not going to deny it, aunt," said Liza, in a scarcely audible voice.

"Ah, ah! Then it is so, my mother. You made an appointment with him, that old sinner, that remarkably sweet creature!"

"No."

"How was it, then?"

"I came down to the drawing-room to look for a book. He was in the garden; and he called me."

"And you went? Very good, indeed! Perhaps you love him, then?"

"I do love him," said Liza quietly.

"Oh, my mothers! She does love him!" Here Marfa Timofeevna took off her cap. "She loves a married man! Eh? Loves him!"

"He had told me—" began Liza.

"What he had told you, this little hawk? Eh, what?"

"He had told me that his wife was dead."

Marfa Timofeevna made the sign of the cross. "The kingdom of heaven be to her," she whispered. "She was a frivolous woman. But don't let's think about that. So that's how it is. I see, he's a widower. Oh yes, he's going ahead. He has killed one wife, and now he's after a second. A nice sort of person he is, to be sure. But, niece, let me tell you this, in my young days things of this kind used to turn out very badly for girls. Don't be angry with me, my mother. It's only tools who are angry with the truth. I've even told them not to let him in to see me to-day. I love him, but I shall never forgive him for this. So he is a widower! Give me some water. But as to your putting Panshine's nose out of joint, why I think you're a good girl for that. But don't go sitting out at night with men creatures. Don't make me wretched in my old age, and remember that I'm not altogether given over to fondling. I can bite, too—A widower!"

Marfa Timofeevna went away, and Liza sat down in a

corner, and cried a long time. Her heart was heavy within her. She had not deserved to be so humiliated. It was not in a joyous manner that love had made itself known to her. It was for the second time since yesterday morning that she was crying now. This new and unlooked-for feeling had only just sprung into life within her heart, and already how deafly had she had to pay for it, how roughly had other hands dealt with her treasured secret! She felt ashamed, and hurt, and unhappy; but neither doubt nor fear troubled her, and Lavretsky became only still dearer to her. She had hesitated so long as she was not sure of her own feelings; but after that interview, after that kiss—she could no longer hesitate. She knew now that she loved, and that she loved earnestly, honestly; she knew that her's was a firm attachment, one which would last for her whole life. As for threats, she did not fear them. She felt that this tie was one which no violence could break.

XXXVII

Maria Dmitrievna was greatly embarrassed when she was informed that Madame Lavretsky was at the door. She did not even know whether she ought to receive her, being afraid of offending Lavretsky; but at last curiosity prevailed. "After all," she thought, "she is a relation, too." So she seated herself in an easy chair, and said to the footman, "Show her in."

A few minutes went by, then the door was thrown open, and Varvara Pavlovna, with a swift and almost noiseless step, came up to Maria Dmitrievna, and, without giving her time to rise from her chair, almost went down upon her knees before her.

"Thank you, aunt," she began in Russian, speaking softly, but in a tone of deep emotion. "Thank you; I had not even dared to hope that you would condescend so far. You are an angel of goodness."

Having said this, Varvara Pavlovna unexpectedly laid hold of one of Maria Dmitrievna's hands, gently pressed it between her pale-lilac Jouvin's gloves, and then lifted it respectfully to her pouting, rosy lips. Maria Dmitrievna was entirely carried away by the sight of such a handsome and exquisitely dressed woman almost at her feet, and did not know what position to assume. She felt half inclined to draw back her hand, half inclined to make her visitor sit down, and to say something affectionate to her. She ended by rising from her chair and kissing Varvara's smooth and perfumed forehead.

Varvara appeared to be totally overcome by that kiss.

"How do you do? *bonjour*," said Maria Dmitrievna. "I never imagined—however, I'm really delighted to see you. You will understand, my dear, it is not my business to be judge between a man and his wife."

"My husband is entirely in the right," said Varvara Pavlovna, interrupting her, "I alone am to blame."

"Those are very praiseworthy sentiments, very," said Maria Dmitrievna. "Is it long since you arrived? Have you seen him? But do sit down."

"I arrived yesterday," answered Varvara Pavlovna, seating herself on a chair in an attitude expressive of humility. "I have seen my husband, and I have spoken with him."

"Ah! Well, and what did he say?"

"I was afraid that my coming so suddenly might make him angry," continued Varvara Pavlovna; "but he did not refuse to see me."

"That is to say, he has not—Yes, yes, I understand," said Maria Dmitrievna. "It is only outwardly that he seems a little rough; his heart is really soft."

"Fedor Ivanovich has not pardoned me. He did not want to listen to me. But he has been good enough to let me have Lavriki to live in."

"Ah, a lovely place!"

"I shall set off there to-morrow, according to his desire. But I considered it a duty to pay you a visit first."

"I am very, very much obliged to you my dear. One ought never to forget one's relations. But do you know I am astonished at your speaking Russian so well. *C'est etonnant.*"

Varvara Pavlovna smiled.

"I have been too long abroad, Maria Dmitrievna, I am well aware of that. But my heart has always been Russian, and I have not forgotten my native land."

"Yes, yes. There's nothing like that. Your husband certainly didn't expect you in the least. Yes, trust my experience—*la patrie avant tout.* Oh! please let me! What a charming mantilla you have on!"

"Do you like it?" Varvara took it quickly off her shoulders. "It is very simple; one of Madame Baudran's."

"One can see that at a glance. How lovely, and in what exquisite taste! I feel sure you've brought a number of charming things with you. How I should like to see them!"

"All my toilette is at your service, dearest aunt. I might show your maid something if you liked. I have brought a maid from Paris, a wonderful needle-woman."

"You are exceedingly good, my dear. But, really, I haven't the conscience—"

"Haven't the conscience!" repeated Varvara Pavlovna, in a reproachful tone. "If you wish to make me happy, you will

Ivan S. Turgenev

dispose of me as if I belonged to you."

Maria Dmitrievna fairly gave way.

"*Vous etes charmante,*" she said. But why don't you take off your bonnet and gloves?"

"What! You allow me?" asked Varvara Pavlovna, gently clasping her hands with an air of deep emotion.

"Of course. You will dine with us, I hope. I—I will introduce my daughter to you." (Maria Dmitrievna felt embarrassed for a moment, but then, "Well, so be it," she thought.) "She happens not to be quite well to-day.'

"Oh! *ma tante,* how kind you are!" exclaimed Varvara Pavlovna, lifting her handkerchief to her eyes.

At this moment the page announced Gedeonovsky's arrival, and the old gossip came in smiling, and bowing profoundly. Maria Dmitrievna introduced him to her visitor. At first he was somewhat abashed, but Varvara Pavlovna behaved to him with such coquettish respectfulness that his ears soon began to tingle, and amiable speeches and gossiping stories began to flow uninterruptedly from his lips.

Varvara Pavlovna listened to him, slightly smiling at times, then by degrees she too began to talk. She spoke in a modest way about Paris, about her travels, about Baden; she made Maria Dmitrievna laugh two or three times, and each time she uttered a gentle sigh afterwards, as if she were secretly reproaching herself for her unbecoming levity; she asked leave to bring Ada to the house; she took off her gloves, and with her smooth white hands she pointed out how and where flounces, ruches, lace, and so forth, were worn; she promised to bring a bottle of new English scent—the Victoria essence—and was as pleased as a child when Maria Dmitrievna consented to accept it as a present; and she melted into tears at the remembrance of the emotion she had experienced when she heard the first Russian bells.

"So profoundly did they sink into my very heart," she said.

At that moment Liza came into the room.

All that day, ever since the moment when, cold with dismay, Liza had read Lavretsky's note, she had been preparing herself for an interview with his wife. She foresaw that she would see her, and she determined not to avoid her, by way of inflicting upon herself a punishment for what she considered her culpable hopes. The unexpected crisis which had taken place in her fate had profoundly shaken her. In the course of about a couple of hours her face seemed to have grown thin. But she had not shed a single tear. "It is what you deserve," she said to herself, repressing, though not without difficulty, and at the cost of considerable agitation, certain bitter thoughts and evil impulses which frightened her as they arose in her mind. "Well, I must go," she thought, as soon as she heard of Madame Lavretsky's arrival, and she went.

She stood outside the drawing-room door for a long time before she could make up her mind to open it At last, saying to herself, "I am guilty before her," she entered the room, and forced herself to look at her, even forced herself to smile. Varvara Pavlovna came forward to meet her as soon as she saw her come in, and made her a slight, but still a respectful salutation.

"Allow me to introduce myself," she began, in an insinuating tone." Your mamma has been so indulgent towards me that I hope that you too will be—good to me."

The expression of Varvara Pavlovna's face as she uttered these last words, her cunning smile, her cold and, at the same time, loving look, the movements of her arms and shoulders, her very dress, her whole being, aroused such a feeling of repugnance in Liza's mind that she absolutely could not answer her, and only by a strong effort could succeed in holding out her hand to her. "This young lady dislikes me," thought Varvara Pavlovna, as she squeezed Liza's cold fingers, then, turning to Maria Dmitrievna, she said in a half whisper. "*Mais elle est delicieuse!*"

Liza faintly reddened. In that exclamation she seemed to detect a tone of irony and insult. However, she determined not to trust to that impression, and she took her seat at her embroidery frame near the window.

Even there Varvara Pavlovna would not leave her in peace. She came to her, and began to praise her cleverness and taste. Liza's heart began to beat with painful force. Scarcely could she master her feelings, scarcely could she remain sitting quietly in her place. It seemed to her as if Varvara Pavlovna knew all and were mocking her with secret triumph. Fortunately for her, Gedeonovsky began to talk to Varvara and diverted her attention. Liza bent over her frame and watched her without being observed. "That woman," she thought, "was once loved by *him*." But then she immediately drove out of her mind even so much as the idea of Lavretsky. She felt her head gradually beginning to swim, and she was afraid of losing command over herself. Maria Dmitrievna began to talk about music.

"I have heard, my dear," she began, "that you are a wonderful *virtuosa*."

"I haven't played for a long time," replied Varvara Pavlovna, but she immediately took her seat at the piano and ran her fingers rapidly along the keys. "Do you wish me to play?"

"If you will do us that favor."

Varvara Pavlovna played in a masterly style a brilliant and difficult study by Herz. Her performance was marked by great power and rapidity.

"*A sylphide!*" exclaimed Gedeonovsky.

"It is wonderful!" declared Maria Dmitrievna. "I must confess you have fairly astonished me, Varvara Pavlovna," calling that lady by her name for the first time. "Why you might give concerts. We have a musician here, an old German, very learned and quite an original. He gives Liza lessons. You would simply make him go out of his mind."

"Is Lizaveta Mikhailovna also a musician?" asked Madame Lavretsky, turning her head a little towards her.

"Yes; she doesn't play badly, and she is very fond I of music. But what does that signify in comparison with you? But we have a young man here besides. You really must make his acquaintance. He is a thorough artist in feeling, and he composes charmingly. He is the only person here who can fully appreciate you"

"A young man?" said Varvara Pavlovna. "What is he? Some poor fellow?"

"I beg your pardon. He is the leading cavalier here, and not here only—*et a Petersbourg*—a chamberlain, received in the best society. You surely must have heard of him—Vladimir Nikolaevich Panshine. He is here on government business— a future minister!"

"And an artist too?"

"An artist in feeling, and so amiable. You shall see him. He has been here a great deal for some time past. I asked him to come this evening. I *hope* he will come," added Maria Dmitrievna with a slight sigh and a bitter smile.

Liza understood the hidden meaning of that smile, but she had other things to think about then.

"And he's young?" repeated Varvara Pavlovna, lightly modulating from key to key.

"Twenty-eight years old—and a most pleasing exterior. *Un jeune homme accompli.*"

"A model young man, one may say," remarked Gedeonovsky.

Varvara Pavlovna suddenly began to play a noisy waltz by Strauss, beginning with so loud and quick a trill that Gedeonovsky fairly started. Right in the middle of the waltz she passed abruptly into a plaintive air, and ended with the *Fra poco* out of *Lucia*. She had suddenly remembered that joyful music was not in keeping with her position.

Maria Dmitrievna was deeply touched by the air from *Lucia*, in which great stress was laid upon the sentimental passages.

"What feeling!" she whispered to Gedeonovsky.

"*A Sylphide!*" repeated Gedeonovsky, lifting his eyes to heaven.

The dinner hour arrived. Marfa Timofeevna did not come down from up-stairs until the soup was already placed on the table. She behaved very coldly to Varvara Pavlovna, answering her amiable speeches with broken phrases, and never even looking at her. Varvara soon perceived that there was no conversation to be got out of that old lady, so she gave up talking to her. On the other hand Madame Kalitine became still more caressing in her behavior towards her guest. She was vexed by her aunt's rudeness.

After all, it was not only Varvara that the old lady would not look at. She did not once look at Liza either, although her eyes almost glowed with a meaning light. Pale, almost yellow, there she sat, with compressed lips, looking as if she were made of stone, and would eat nothing.

As for Liza, she seemed calm, and was so in reality. Her heart was quieter than it had been. A strange callousness, the callousness of the condemned, had come over her.

During dinner Varvara Pavlovna said little. She seemed to have become timid again, and her face wore an expression of modest melancholy. Gedeonovsky was the only person who kept the conversation alive, relating several of his stories, though from time to time he looked timidly at Marfa Timofeevna and coughed. That cough always seized him whenever he was going to embellish the truth in her presence. But this time she did not meddle with him, never once interrupted him.

After dinner it turned out that Varvara Pavlovna was very fond of the game of preference. Madame Kalitine was so pleased at this that she felt quite touched and inwardly thought, "Why, what a fool Fedor Ivanovich must be! Fancy not having been able to comprehend such a woman!"

She sat down to cards with Varvara and Gedeonov sky; but Marfa Timofeevna carried off Liza to her room up-stairs, saying that the girl "had no face left," and she was sure her head must be aching.

"Yes, her head aches terribly," said Madame Kalitine, addressing Varvara Pavlovna, and rolling her eyes. "I often have such headaches myself."

"Really!" answered Varvara Pavlovna.

Liza entered her aunt's room, and sank on a chair perfectly worn out. For a long time Marfa Timofeevna looked at her in silence, then she quietly knelt down before her, and began, still quite silently, to kiss her hands—first one, and then the other.

Liza bent forwards and reddened—then she began to cry; but she did not make her aunt rise, nor did she withdraw her hands from her. She felt that she had no right to withdraw them—had no right to prevent the old lady from expressing her sorrow, her sympathy—from asking to be pardoned for what had taken place the day before. And Marfa Timofeevna could not sufficiently kiss those poor, pale, nerveless hands; while silent tears poured down from her eyes and from Liza's too. And the cat, Matros, purred in the large chair by the side of the stocking and the ball of worsted; the long, thin flame of the little lamp feebly wavered in front of the holy picture; and in the next room, just the other side of the door, stood Nastasia Carpovna, and furtively wiped her eyes with a check pocket-handkerchief, rolled up into a sort of ball.

XXXVIII

Down-stairs, meanwhile, the game of preference went on. Maria Dmitrievna was winning, and was in a very good humor. A servant entered and announced Panshine's arrival. Maria Dmitrievna let fall her cards, and fidgeted in her chair. Varvara Pavlovna looked at her with a half-smile, and then turned her eyes towards the door.

Panshine appeared in a black dress-coat, buttoned all the way up, and wearing a high English shirt-collar. "It was painful for me to obey; but, you see, I have come;" that was what was expressed by his serious face, evidently just shaved for the occasion.

"Why, Valdemar!" exclaimed Maria Dmitrievna, "you used always to come in without being announced."

Panshine made no other reply than a look, and bowed politely to Maria Dmitrievna, but did not kiss her hand. She introduced him to Varvara Pavlovna. He drew back a pace, bowed to her with the same politeness and with an added expression of respectful grace, and then took a seat at the card-table. The game soon came to an end. Panshine asked after Lizaveta Mikhailovna, and expressed his regret at hearing that she was not quite well. Then he began to converse with Varvara Pavlovna, weighing every word

Ivan S. Turgenev

carefully and emphasizing it distinctly in true diplomatic style, and, when she spoke, respectfully hearing her answers to the end. But the seriousness of his diplomatic tone produced no effect upon Varvara Pavlovna, who would have nothing to do with it. On the contrary, she looked him full in the face with a sort of smiling earnestness, and in talking with him seemed thoroughly at her ease, while her delicate nostrils lightly quivered, as though with suppressed laughter.

Maria Dmitrievna began to extol Varvara's cleverness. Panshine bent his head politely, as far as his shirt-collar permitted him, declared that he had already been convinced of the exceptional nature of her talents, and all but brought round the conversation to the subject of Metternich himself. Varvara Pavlovna half-closed her velvety eyes, and, having said in a low voice, "But you are an artist also, *un confrere*," added still lower, "*Venez*!" and made a sign with her head in the direction of the piano. This single word, "*Venez*!" so abruptly spoken, utterly changed Panshine's appearance, as if by magic, in a single moment. His care-worn air disappeared, he began to smile, he became animated, he unbuttoned his coat, and, saying "I am an artist! Not at all; but you, I hear, are an artist indeed," he followed Varvara Pavlovna to the piano.

"Tell him to sing the romance, 'How the moon floats,'" exclaimed Maria Dmitrievna.

"You sing?" asked Varvara Pavlovna, looking at him with a bright and rapid glance. "Sit down there."

Panshine began to excuse himself.

"Sit down," she repeated, tapping the back of the chair in a determined manner.

He sat down, coughed, pulled up his shirt-collar, and sang his romance.

"*Charmant*," said Varvara Pavlovna. "You sing admirably— *vous avez du style*. Sing it again."

She went round to the other side of the piano, and placed herself exactly opposite Panshine. He repeated his romance, giving a melodramatic variation to his voice. Varvara looked at him steadily, resting her elbows on the piano, with her white hands on a level with her lips. The song ended, "*Charmant! Charmante idee*," she said, with the quiet confidence of a connoisseur. "Tell me, have you written anything for a woman's voice—a mezzo-soprano?"

"I scarcely write anything," answered Panshine. "I do so only now and then—between business hours. But do you sing?"

"Oh yes! do sing us something," said Maria Dmitrievna.

Varvara Pavlovna tossed her head, and pushed her hair back from her flushed cheeks. Then, addressing Panshine, she said—

"Our voices ought to go well together. Let us sing a duet. Do you know '*Son geloso*,' or '*La ci darem*,' or '*Mira la bianca luna*?'"

"I used to sing '*Mira la bianca luna*,'" answered Panshine; but it was a long time ago. I have forgotten it now."

"Never mind, we will hum it over first by way of experiment. Let me come there."

Varvara Pavlovna sat down to the piano. Panshine stood by her side. They hummed over the duet, Varvara Pavlovna correcting him several times; then they sang it out loud, and afterwards repeated it twice—"*Mira la bianca lu-u-una.*" Varvara's voice had lost its freshness, but she managed it with great skill. At first Panshine was nervous, and sang rather false, but afterwards he experienced an artistic glow; and, if he did not sing faultlessly, at all events he shrugged his shoulders, swayed his body to and fro, and from time to time lifted his hand aloft, like a genuine vocalist.

Varvara Pavlovna afterwards played two or three little pieces by Thalberg, and coquettishly chanted a French song. Maria Dmitrievna did not know how to express her delight, and several times she felt inclined to send for Liza. Gedeonovsky, too, could not find words worthy of the occasion, and could only shake his head. Suddenly, however, and quite unexpectedly, he yawned, and only just contrived to hide his mouth with his hand.

That yawn did not escape Varvara's notice. She suddenly turned her back upon the piano, saying, "*Assez de musique comme ca*; let us talk a little," and crossed her hands before her.

"*Oui, asses de musique,*" gladly repeated Panshine, and began a conversation with her—a brisk and airy conversation, carried on in French. "Exactly as if it were in one of the best Paris drawing-rooms," thought Maria Dmitrievna, listening to their quick and supple talk.

Panshine felt completely happy. He smiled, and his eyes shone. At first, when he happened to meet Maria Dmitrievna's eyes, he would pass his hand across his face and frown and sigh abruptly, but after a time he entirely forgot her presence, and gave himself up unreservedly to the enjoyment of a half-fashionable, half-artistic chat.

Varvara Pavlovna proved herself a great philosopher. She had an answer ready for everything; she doubted nothing; she did not hesitate at anything. It was evident that she had talked often and much with all kinds of clever people. All her thoughts and feelings circled around Paris. When Panshine made literature the subject of the conversation, it turned out that she, like him, had read nothing but French books. George Sand irritated her; Balzac she esteemed, although he wearied her; to Eugene Sue and Scribe she ascribed a profound knowledge of the human heart; Dumas and Feval she adored. In reality she preferred Paul de Kock to all the others; but, as may be supposed, she did not even mention his name. To tell the truth, literature did not interest her overmuch.

Varvara Pavlovna avoided with great skill every thing that might, even remotely, allude to her position. In all that she said, there was not even the slightest mention made of love; on the contrary, her language seemed rather to express an austere feeling with regard to the allurements of the passions, and to breathe the accents of disillusionment and resignation.

Panshine replied to her, but she refused to agree with him. Strange to say, however, at the very time when she was uttering words which conveyed what was frequently a harsh judgment, the accents of those very words were tender and caressing, and her eyes expressed—What those charming eyes expressed it would be hard to say, but it was something which had no harshness about it, rather a mysterious sweetness. Panshine tried to make out their hidden meaning, tried to make his own eyes eloquent, but he was conscious that he failed. He acknowledged that Varvara Pavlovna, in her capacity as a real lioness from abroad, stood on a higher level than he; and, therefore, he was not altogether master of himself.

Varvara Pavlovna had a habit of every now and then just touching the sleeve of the person with whom she was conversing. These light touches greatly agitated Panshine. She had the faculty of easily becoming intimate with any one. Before a couple of hours had passed, it seemed to Panshine as if he had known her an age, and as if Liza—that very Liza whom he had loved so much, and to whom he had proposed the evening before—had vanished in a kind of fog.

Tea was brought; the conversation became even more free from restraint than before. Madame Kalitine rang for the page, and told him to ask Liza to come down if her headache was better. At the sound of Liza's name, Panshine began to talk about self-sacrifice, and to discuss the question as to which is the more capable of such sacrifice—man or woman. Maria Dmitrievna immediately became excited, began to affirm that the woman is the more capable, asserted that she could prove the fact in a few words, got confused over them, and ended with a sufficiently unfortunate comparison. Varvara Pavlovna took up a sheet of music, and half-screening her face with it, bent over towards Panshine, and said in a whisper, while she nibbled a biscuit, a quiet smile playing about her lips and her eyes, "*Elle n'a pas invente la poudre, la bonne dame.*"

Panshine was somewhat astonished, and a little alarmed by Varvara's audacity, but he did not detect the amount of contempt for himself that lay hid in that unexpected sally, and—forgetting all Maria Dmitrievna's kindness and her attachment towards him, forgetting the dinners she had given him, the money she had lent him—he replied (unhappy mortal that he was) in the same tone, and with a similar smile, "*Je crois bien!*" and what is more he did not even say "*Je crois bien!*" but "*J'crois ben!*"

Varvara Pavlovna gave him a friendly look, and rose from

her seat. At that moment Liza entered the room. Marfa Timofeevna had tried to prevent her going but in vain. Liza was resolved to endure her trial to the end. Varvara Pavlovna advanced to meet her, attended by Panshine, whose face again wore its former diplomatic expression.

"How are you now?" asked Varvara.

"I am better now, thank you," replied Liza.

"We have been passing the time with a little music," said Panshine. "It is a pity you did not hear Varvara Pavlovna. She sings charmingly, *en artiste consommee*."

"Come here, *ma chere*," said Madame Kalitine's voice.

With childlike obedience, Varvara immediately went to her, and sat down on a stool at her feet. Maria Dmitrievna had called her away, in order that she might leave her daughter alone with Panshine, if only for a moment. She still hoped in secret that Liza would change her mind. Besides this, an idea had come into her mind, which she wanted by all means to express.

"Do you know," she whispered to Varvara Pavlovna, "I want to try and reconcile you and your husband. I cannot promise to succeed, but I will try. He esteems me very much, you know."

Varvara slowly looked up at Maria Dmitrievna, and gracefully clasped her hands together.

"You would be my saviour, *ma tante*," she said, with a sad voice. "I don't know how to thank you properly for all your kindness; but I am too guilty before Fedor Ivanovich. He cannot forgive me."

"But did you actually—in reality—?" began Maria Dmitrievna, with lively curiosity.

"Do not ask me," said Varvara, interrupting her, and then looked down. "I was young, light headed—However, I don't wish to make excuses for myself."

"Well, in spite of all that, why not make the attempt? Don't give way to despair," replied Maria Dmitrievna, and was going to tap her on the cheek, but looked at her, and was afraid. "She is modest and discreet," she thought, "but, for all that, a *lionne* still!"

"Are you unwell?" asked Panshine, meanwhile.

"I am not quite well," replied Liza.

"I understand," he said, after rather a long silence, "Yes, I understand."

"What do you mean?"

"I understand," significantly repeated Panshine, who simply was at a loss for something to say.

Liza felt confused, but then she thought, "What does it matter?"

Meanwhile Panshine assumed an air of mystery and maintained silence, looking in a different direction with a grave expression on his face.

"Why I fancy it must be past eleven!" observed Maria Dmitrievna. Her guests understood the hint and began to take leave. Varvara was obliged to promise to come and dine to-morrow, and to bring Ada with her. Gedeonovsky, who had all but gone to sleep as he sat in a corner, offered to escort her home. Panshine bowed gravely to all the party; afterwards, as he stood on the steps after seeing Varvara into her carriage, he gave her hand a gentle pressure, and exclaimed, as she drove away, "*Au revoir*!" Gedeonovsky sat by her side in the carriage, and all the way home she amused herself by putting the tip of her little foot, as if by accident, on his foot. He felt abashed, and tried to make her complimentary speeches. She tittered, and made eyes at him when the light from the street lamps shone Into the carriage. The waltz she had played rang in her ears and excited her. Wherever she might be she had only to imagine a ballroom and a blaze of light, and swift circling round to the sound of music, and her heart would burn within her, her eyes would glow with a strange lustre, a smile would wander around her lips, a kind of bacchanalian grace would seem to diffuse itself over her whole body.

When they arrived at her house Varvara lightly bounded from the carriage, as only a *lionne* could bound, turned towards Gedeonovsky, and suddenly burst out laughing in his face.

"A charming creature," thought the councillor of state, as he made his way home to his lodgings, where his servant was waiting for him with a bottle of opodeldoc. "It's as well that I'm a steady man—But why did she laugh?"

All that night long Marfa Timofeevna sat watching by Liza's bedside.

XXXIX

Lavretsky spent a day and a half at Vasilievskoe, wandering about the neighborhood almost all the time. He could not remain long in any one place. His grief goaded him on. He experienced all the pangs of a ceaseless, impetuous, and impotent longing. He remembered the feeling which had come over him the day after his first arrival. He remembered the resolution he had formed then, and he felt angrily indignant with himself. What was it that had been able to wrest him aside from that which he had acknowledged as his duty, the single problem of his future life? The thirst after happiness—the old thirst after happiness. "It seems that Mikhalevich was right after all," he thought. "You wanted to find happiness in life once more," he said to himself. "You forgot that for happiness to visit a man even once is an undeserved favor, a steeping in luxury. Your happiness was incomplete—was false, you may say. Well, show what right you have to true and complete happiness! Look around you and see who is happy, who enjoys his life! There is a peasant going to the field to mow. It may be that he is satisfied with his lot. But what of that? Would you be willing to exchange lots with him? Remember your own mother. How exceedingly modest were her wishes, and yet what sort of a lot fell to her share! You seem to have only been boasting before Panshine, when you told him that you had come into Russia to till the soil. It was to run after the girls in your old age that you came. Tidings of freedom, reached you, and you flung aside every thing, forgot every thing, ran like a child after a butterfly."

In the midst of his reflections the image of Liza constantly haunted him. By a violent effort he tried to drive it away, and along with it another haunting face, other beautiful but ever malignant and hateful features.

Old Anton remarked that his master was not quite himself; and after sighing several times behind the door, and several times on the threshold, he ventured to go up to him, and advised him to drink something hot. Lavretsky spoke to him harshly, and ordered him out of the room: afterwards he told the old man he was sorry he had done so; but this only made Anton sadder than he had been before.

Lavretsky could not stop in the drawing-room. He fancied that his great grandfather, Andrei, was looking out from his frame with contempt on his feeble descendant. "So much for you! You float in shallow water!"[A] the wry lips seemed to be saying to him. "Is it possible," he thought, "that I cannot gain mastery over myself; that I am going to yield to this— this trifling affair!" (Men who are seriously wounded in a battle always think their wounds "a mere trifle;" when a man can deceive himself no longer, it is time to give up living). "Am I really a child? Well, yes I have seen near at hand, I have almost grasped, the possibility of gaining a life-long happiness—and then it has suddenly disappeared. It is just the same in a lottery. Turn the wheel a little more, and the pauper would perhaps be rich. If it is not to be, it is not to be—and all is over. I will betake me to my work with set teeth, and I will force myself to be silent; and I shall succeed, for it is not for the first time that I take myself in hand. And why have I run away? Why do I stop here, vainly hiding my head, like an ostrich? Misfortune a terrible thing to look in the face! Nonsense!"

[Footnote A: See note to page 142.]

"Anton!" he called loudly, "let the tarantass be got ready immediately."

"Yes," he said to himself again. "I must compel myself to be silent; I must keep myself tightly in hand."

With such reflections as these Lavretsky sought to assuage his sorrow; but it remained as great and as bitter as before. Even Apraxia, who had outlived, not only her intelligence, but almost all her faculties, shook her head, and followed him with sad eyes as he started in the tarantass for the town. The horses galloped. He sat erect and motionless, and looked straight along the road.

XL

Liza had written to Lavretsky the night before telling him to come and see her on this evening; but he went to his own house first. He did not find either his wife or his daughter there; and the servant told him that they had both gone to the Kalitines'! This piece of news both annoyed and enraged him. "Varvara Pavlovna seems to be determined not to let me live in peace," he thought, an angry feeling stirring in his heart. He began walking up and down the room, pushing away every moment, with hand or foot, one of the toys or books or feminine belongings which fell in his way. Then he called Justine, and told her to take away all that "rubbish."

"*Oui, monsieur,*" she replied, with a grimace, and began to set the room in order, bending herself into graceful attitudes, and by each of her gestures making Lavretsky feel that she considered him an uncivilized bear. It was with a sensation of downright hatred that he watched the mocking expression of her faded, but still *piquante*, Parisian face, and looked at her white sleeves, her silk apron, and her little cap. At last he sent her away, and, after long hesitation, as Varvara Pavlovna did not return, he determined to go to the Kalitines', and pay a visit, not to Madame Kalitine (for nothing would have induced him to enter her drawing-room—that drawing-room in which his wife was), but to Marfa Timofeevna. He remembered that a back staircase, used by the maid-servants, led straight to her room.

Lavretsky carried out his plan. By a fortunate chance he met Shurochka in the court-yard, and she brought him to Marfa Timofeevna. He found the old lady, contrary to her usual custom, alone. She was without her cap, and was sitting in a corner of the room in a slouching attitude, her arms folded across her breast. When she saw Lavretsky, she was much agitated, and jumping up hastily from her chair, she began going here and there about the room, as if she were looking for her cap.

"Ah! so you have come, then," she said, fussing about and avoiding his eyes. "Well, good day to you! Well, what's— what's to be done? Where were you yesterday? Well, she has come. Well—yes. Well, it must be—somehow or other."

Lavretsky sank upon a chair.

"Well, sit down, sit down," continued the old lady. "Did you come straight up-stairs? Yes, of course. Eh! You came to see after me? Many thanks."

The old lady paused. Lavretsky did not know what to say to her; but she understood him.

"Liza—yes; Liza was here just now," she continued tying and untying the strings of her work-bag. "She isn't quite well. Shurochka, where are you? Come here, my mother; cannot you sit still a moment? And I have a headache myself. It must be that singing which has given me it, and the music."

"What singing, aunt?"

"What? don't you know? They have already begun—what do you call them?—duets down there. And all in Italian—chi-

chi and cha-cha—regular magpies. With their long drawn-out notes, one would think they were going to draw one's soul out. It's that Panshine, and your wife too. And how quickly it was all arranged! Quite without ceremony, just as if among near relations. However, one must say that even a dog will try to find itself a home somewhere. You needn't die outside if folks don't chase you away from their houses."

"I certainly must confess I did not expect this," answered Lavretsky. "This must have required considerable daring."

"No, my dear, it isn't daring with her, it is calculation. However, God be with her! They say you are going to send her to Lavriki. Is that true?"

"Yes; I am going to make over that property to her."

"Has she asked you for money?"

"Not yet."

"Well, that request won't be long in coming. But—I haven't looked at you till now—are you well?"

"Quite well."

"Shurochka!" suddenly exclaimed the old lady. "Go and tell Lizaveta Mikhailovna—that is—no—ask her—Is she downstairs?"

"Yes."

"Well, yes. Ask her where she has put my book She will know all about it."

"Very good."

The old lady commenced bustling about again, and began to open the drawers in her commode. Lavretsky remained quietly sitting on his chair.

Suddenly light steps were heard on the staircase—and Liza entered.

Lavretsky stood up and bowed. Liza remained near the door.

"Liza, Lizochka," hurriedly began Marfa Timofeevna, "where have you—where have you put my book?"

"What book, aunt?"

"Why, good gracious! that book. However, I didn't send for you—but it's all the same. What are you all doing down-stairs? Here is Fedor Ivanovich come. How is your headache?"

"It's of no consequence."

"You always say, 'It's of no consequence.' What are you all doing down below?—having music again?"

"No—They are playing cards."

"Of course; she is ready for anything. Shurochka, I see you want to run out into the garden. Be off!"

"No, I don't Marfa Timofeevna—"

"No arguing, if you please. Be off. Nastasia Carpovna has gone into the garden by herself. Go and keep her company. You should show the old lady respect."

Shurochka left the room.

"But where is my cap? Wherever can it have got to?"

"Let me look for it," said Liza.

"Sit still, sit still! My own legs haven't dropped off yet. It certainly must be in my bed-room."

And Marfa Timofeevna went away, after casting a side-glance at Lavretsky. At first she left the door open, but suddenly she returned and shut it again from the outside.

Liza leant back in her chair and silently hid her face in her hands.

Lavretsky remained standing where he was.

"This is how we have had to see each other!" he said at last.

Liza let her hands fall from before her face.

"Yes," she replied sadly, "we have soon been punished."

"Punished!" echoed Lavretsky. "For what have you, at all events, been punished?"

Liza looked up at him. Her eyes did not express either sorrow or anxiety; but they seemed to have become smaller and dimmer than they used to be. Her face was pale; even her slightly-parted lips had lost their color.

Lavretsky's heart throbbed with pity and with love.

"You have written to me that all is over," he whispered. "Yes, all is over—before it had begun."

"All that must be forgotten," said Liza. "I am glad you have come. I was going to write to you; but it is better as it is. Only we must make the most of these few minutes. Each of us has a duty to fulfil. You, Fedor Ivanovich, must become reconciled with your wife."

"Liza!"

"I entreat you to let it be so. By this alone can expiation be made for—for all that has taken place. Think over it, and then you will not refuse my request."

"Liza! for God's sake! You ask what is impossible. I am ready to do every thing you tell me; but to be reconciled with her *now*!—I consent to every thing, I have forgotten every thing; but I cannot do violence to my heart. Have some pity; this is cruel!"

"But I do not ask you to do what is impossible. Do not live with her if you really cannot do so. But be reconciled with her," answered Liza, once more hiding her face in her hands. "Remember your daughter; and, besides, do it for my sake."

"Very good," said Lavretsky between his teeth. "Suppose I do this—in this I shall be fulfilling my duty; well, but you—in what does your duty consist?"

"That I know perfectly well."

Lavretsky suddenly shuddered.

"Surely you have not made up your mind to many Panshine?" he asked.

"Oh, no!" replied Liza, with an almost imperceptible smile.

"Ah! Liza, Liza!" exclaimed Lavretsky, "how happy we

might have been!"

Liza again looked up at him.

"Now even you must see, Fedor Ivanovich, that happiness does not depend upon ourselves, but upon God."

"Yes, because you—"

The door of the next room suddenly opened, and Marfa Timofeevna came in, holding her cap in her hand.

"I had trouble enough to find it," she said, standing between Liza and Lavretsky; "I had stuffed it away myself. Dear me, see what old age comes to! But, after all, youth is no better. Well, are you going to Lavriki with your wife?" she added, turning to Fedor Ivanovich.

"To Lavriki with her? I?—I don't know," he added, after a short pause.

"Won't you pay a visit down stairs?"

"Not to-day."

"Well, very good; do as you please. But you, Liza, ought to go down-stairs, I think. Ah! my dears. I've forgotten to give any seed to my bullfinch too. Wait a minute; I will be back directly."

And Marfa Timofeevna ran out of the room without even having put on her cap.

Lavretsky quickly drew near to Liza.

"Liza," he began, with an imploring voice, "we are about to

part for ever, and my heart is very heavy. Give me your hand at parting."

Liza raised her head. Her wearied, almost lustre less eyes looked at him steadily.

"No," she said, and drew back the hand she had half held out to him. "No, Lavretsky" (it was the first time that she called him by this name), "I will not give you my hand. Why should I? And now leave me, I beseech you. You know that I love you—Yes, I love you!" she added emphatically. "But no—no;" and she raised her handkerchief to her lips.

"At least, then, give me that handkerchief—"

The door creaked. The handkerchief glided down to Liza's knees. Lavretsky seized it before it had time to fall on the floor, and quickly hid it away in his pocket; then, as he turned round, he encountered the glance of Marfa Timofeevna's eyes.

"Lizochka, I think your mother is calling you," said the old lady.

Liza immediately got up from her chair, and left the room.

Marfa Timofeevna sat down again in her corner, Lavretsky was going to take leave of her.

"Fedia," she said, abruptly.

"What, Aunt?"

"Are you an honorable man?"

"What?"

"I ask you—Are you an honorable man?"

"I hope so."

"Hm! Well, then, give me your word that you are going to behave like an honorable man."

"Certainly. But why do you ask that?"

"I know why, perfectly well. And so do you, too, my good friend.[A] As you are no fool, you will understand why I ask you this, if you will only think over it a little. But now, good-bye, my dear. Thank you for coming to see me; but remember what I have said, Fedia; and now give me a kiss. Ah, my dear, your burden is heavy to bear, I know that. But no one finds his a light one. There was a time when I used to envy the flies. There are creatures, I thought, who live happily in the world. But one night I heard a fly singing out under a spider's claws. So, thought I, even they have their troubles. What can be done, Fedia? But mind you never forget what you have said to me. And now leave me—leave me."

[Footnote A: Literally, "my foster father," or "my benefactor."]

Lavretsky left by the back door, and had almost reached the street, when a footman ran after him and said, "Maria Dmitrievna told me to ask you to come to her."

"Tell her I cannot come just now," began Lavretsky.

"She told me to ask you particularly," continued the footman. "She told me to say that she was alone."

"Then her visitors have gone away?" asked Lavretsky.

"Yes," replied the footman, with something like a grin on his face.

Lavretsky shrugged his shoulders, and followed him into the house.

XLI

Maria Dmitrievna was alone in her boudoir. She was sitting in a large easy-chair, sniffing Eau-de-Cologne, with a little table by her side, on which was a glass containing orange-flower water. She was evidently excited, and seemed nervous about something.

Lavretsky came into the room.

"You wanted to see me," he said, bowing coldly.

"Yes," answered Maria Dmitrievna, and then she drank a little water. "I heard that you had gone straight up-stairs to my aunt, so I told the servants to ask you to come and see me. I want to have a talk with you. Please sit down."

Maria Dmitrievna took breath. "You know that your wife has come," she continued.

"I am aware of that fact," said Lavretsky.

"Well—yes—that is—I meant to say that she has been here, and I have received her. That is what I wanted to have the explanation about with you, Fedor Ivanovich, I have deserved, I may say, general respect, thank God! and I wouldn't, for all the world, do any thing unbecoming. But, although I saw beforehand that it would be disagreeable to you, Fedor Ivanich, yet I couldn't make up my mind to refuse her. She is a relation of mine—through you. Only put yourself into my position. What right had I to shut my door in her face? Surely you must agree with me."

"You are exciting yourself quite unnecessarily, Maria Dmitrievna," replied Lavretsky. "You have done what is perfectly right. I am not in the least angry. I never intended to deprive my wife of the power of seeing her acquaintances. I did not come to see you to-day simply because I did not wish to meet her. That was all."

"Ah! how glad I am to hear you say that, Fedor Ivanich!" exclaimed Maria Dmitrievna. "However, I always expected as much from your noble feelings. But as to my being excited, there's no wonder in that. I am a woman and a mother. And your wife—of course I cannot set myself up as a judge between you and her, I told her so herself; but she is such a charming person that no one can help being pleased with her."

Lavretsky smiled and twirled his hat in his hands.

"And there is something else that I wanted to say to you, Fedor Ivanich," continued Maria Dmitrievna, drawing a little nearer to him. "If you had only seen how modestly, how respectfully she behaved! Really it was perfectly touching. And if you had only heard how she spoke of you! 'I,' she said, 'am altogether guilty before him.' 'I,' she said, 'was not able to appreciate him.' 'He,' she said, 'is an angel, not a mere man,' I can assure you that's what she said—'an angel.' She is so penitent—I do solemnly declare I have never seen any one so penitent."

"But tell me, Maria Dmitrievna," said Lavretsky, "if I may be allowed to be so inquisitive. I hear that Varvara Pavlovna has been singing here. Was it in one of her penitent moments that she sang, or how—?"

"How can you talk like that and not feel ashamed of yourself? She played and sang simply to give me pleasure, and because I particularly entreated her, almost ordered her to do so. I saw that she was unhappy, so unhappy, and I thought how I could divert her a little; and besides that, I had heard that she had so much talent. Do show her some pity, Fedor Ivanich—she is utterly crushed—only ask Gedeo-novsky—broken down entirely, *tout-a-fait*. How can you say such things of her?"

Lavretsky merely shrugged his shoulders.

"And besides, what a little angel your Adochka is! What a charming little creature! How pretty she is! and how good! and how well she speaks French! And she knows Russian too. She called me aunt in Russian. And then as to shyness, you know, almost all children of her age are shy; but she is not at all so. It's wonderful how like you she is, Fedor Ivanich—eyes, eyebrows, in fact you all over—absolutely you. I don't usually like such young children, I must confess, but I am quite in love with your little daughter."

"Maria Dmitrievna," abruptly said Lavretsky, "allow me to inquire why you are saying all this to me?"

"Why?"—Maria Dmitrievna again had recourse to her Eau-de-Cologne and drank some water—"why I say this to you, Fedor Ivanich, is because—you see I am one of your relations, I take a deep interest in you. I know your heart is excellent. Mark my words, *mon cousin*—at all events I am a woman of experience, and I do not speak at random. Forgive, do forgive your wife!". (Maria Dmitrievna's eyes suddenly filled with tears.) "Only think—youth, inexperience, and perhaps also a bad example—hers was not the sort of mother to put her in the right way. Forgive her, Fedor Ivanich! She has been punished enough."

The tears flowed down Maria Dmitrievna's cheeks. She did not wipe them away; she was fond of weeping. Meanwhile Lavretsky sat as if on thorns. "Good God!" he thought, "what torture this is! What a day this has been for me!"

"You do not reply," Maria Dmitrievna recommenced: "how am I to understand you? Is it possible that you can be so cruel? No, I cannot believe that. I feel that my words have convinced you. Fedor Ivanich, God will reward you for your goodness! Now from my hands receive your wife!"

Lavretsky jumped up from his chair scarcely knowing what he was doing. Maria Dmitrievna had risen also, and had passed rapidly to the other side of the screen, from behind which she brought out Madame Lavretsky. Pale, half lifeless, with downcast eyes, that lady seemed as if she had surrendered her whole power of thinking or willing for herself, and had given herself over entirely into the hands of Maria Dmitrievna.

Lavretsky recoiled a pace.

"You have been there all this time!" he exclaimed.

"Don't blame her," Maria Dmitrievna hastened to say. "She wouldn't have stayed for any thing; but I made her stay; I put her behind the screen. She declared that it would make you angrier than ever; but I wouldn't even listen to her. I know you better than she does. Take then from my hands your wife! Go to him, Varvara; have no fear; fall at your husband's feet" (here she gave Varvara's arm a pull), "and may my blessing—"

"Stop, Maria Dmitrievna!" interposed Lavretsky, in a voice shaking with emotion. "You seem to like sentimental scenes." (Lavretsky was not mistaken; from her earliest school-days Maria Dmitrievna had always been passionately fond of a touch of stage effect.) "They may amuse you, but to other people they may prove very unpleasant. However, I am not going to talk to you. In *this* scene you do not play the leading part."

"What is it *you* want from me, Madame?" he added, turning to his wife. "Have I not done for you all that I could? Do not tell me that it was not you who got up this scene. I should not believe you. You know that I cannot believe you. What is it you want? You are clever. You do nothing without an object. You must feel that to live with you, as I used formerly to live, is what I am not in a position to do—not because I am angry with you, but because I have become a different man. I told you that the very day you returned; and at that time you agreed with me in your own mind. But, perhaps, you wish to rehabilitate yourself in public opinion. Merely to live in my house is too little for you; you want to live with me under the same roof. Is it not so?"

"I want you to pardon me," replied Varvara Pavlovna, without lifting her eyes from the ground.

"She wants you to pardon her," repeated Maria Dmitrievna.

"And not for my own sake, but for Ada's," whispered Varvara.

"Not for her own sake, but for your Ada's," repeated Maria Dmitrievna.

Ivan S. Turgenev

"Very good! That is what you want?" Lavretsky just managed to say. "Well, I consent even to that."

Varvara Pavlovna shot a quick glance at him. Maria Dmitrievna exclaimed, "Thank God!" again took Varvara by the arm, and again began, "Take, then, from my hands—"

"Stop, I tell you!" broke in Lavretsky. "I will consent to live with you, Varvara Pavlovna," he continued; "that is to say, I will take you to Lavriki, and live with you as long as I possibly can. Then I will go away; but I will visit you from time to time. You see, I do not wish to deceive you; only do not ask for more than that. You would laugh yourself, if I were to fulfil the wish of our respected relative, and press you to my heart—if I were to assure you that—that the past did not exist, that the felled tree would again produce leaves. But I see this plainly—one must submit. These words do not convey the same meaning to you as to me, but that does not matter. I repeat, I will live with you—or, no, I cannot promise that; but I will no longer avoid you; I will look on you as my wife again—"

"At all events, give her your hand on that," said Maria Dmitrievna, whose tears had dried up long ago.

"I have never yet deceived Varvara Pavlovna," answered Lavretsky. "She will believe me as it is. I will take her to Lavriki. But remember this, Varvara Pavlovna. Our treaty will be considered at an end, as soon as you give up stopping there. And now let me go away."

He bowed to both of the ladies, and went out quickly.

"Won't you take her with you?" Maria Dmitrievna called after him.

"Let him alone," said Varvara to her in a whisper, and then began to express her thanks to her, throwing her arms around her, kissing her hand, saying she had saved her.

Maria Dmitrievna condescended to accept her caresses, but in reality she was not contented with her; nor was she contented with Lavretsky, nor with the whole scene which she had taken so much pains to arrange. There had been nothing sentimental about it.

According to her ideas Varvara Pavlovna ought to have thrown herself at her husband's feet.

"How was it you didn't understand what I meant?" she kept saying. "Surely I said to you, 'Down with you!'"

"It is better as it is, my dear aunt. Don't disturb yourself—all has turned out admirably," declared Varvara Pavlovna.

"Well, anyhow he is—as cold as ice," said Maria Dmitrievna. "It is true you didn't cry, but surely my tears flowed before his eyes. So he wants to shut you up at Lavriki. What! You won't be able to come out even to see me! All men are unfeeling," she ended by saying, and shook her head with an air of deep meaning.

"But at all events women can appreciate goodness and generosity," said Varvara Pavlovna. Then, slowly sinking on her knees, she threw her arms around Maria Dmitrievna's full waist, and hid her face in that lady's lap. That hidden face wore a smile, but Maria Dmitrievna's tears began to flow afresh.

As for Lavretsky, he returned home, shut himself up in his valet's room, flung himself on the couch, and lay there till the morning.

XLII

The next day was Sunday. Lavretsky was not awakened by the bells which clanged for early Mass, for he had not closed his eyes all night; but they reminded him of another Sunday, when he went to church at Liza's request. He rose in haste. A certain secret voice told him that to-day also he would see her there. He left the house quietly, telling the servant to say to Varvara Pavlovna, who was still asleep, that he would be back to dinner, and then, with long steps, he went where the bell called him with its dreary uniformity of sound.

He arrived early; scarcely any one was yet in the church. A Reader was reciting the Hours in the choir. His voice, sometimes interrupted by a cough, sounded monotonously, rising and falling by turns. Lavretsky placed himself at a little distance from the door. The worshippers arrived, one after another, stopped, crossed themselves, and bowed in all directions. Their steps resounded loudly through the silent and almost empty space, and echoed along the vaulted roof. An infirm old woman, wrapped in a threadbare hooded cloak, knelt by Lavretsky's side and prayed fervently. Her toothless, yellow, wrinkled face expressed intense emotion. Her bloodshot eyes gazed upwards, without moving, on the holy figures displayed upon the iconostasis. Her bony hand kept incessantly coming out from under her cloak, and making the sign of the cross—with a slow and sweeping gesture, and with steady pressure of the fingers on the forehead and the body. A peasant with a morose and thickly-bearded face, his hair and clothes all in disorder, came into the church, threw himself straight down on his knees, and immediately began crossing and prostrating himself, throwing back his head and shaking it after each inclination. So bitter a grief showed itself in his face and in all his gestures, that Lavretsky went up to him and asked him what was the matter. The peasant sank back with an air of distrust; then, looking at him coldly, said in a hurried voice, "My son is dead," and again betook himself to his prostrations.

"What sorrow can they have too great to defy the consolations of the Church?" thought Lavretsky, and he tried to pray himself. But his heart seemed heavy and hardened, and his thoughts were afar off. He kept waiting for Liza; but Liza did not come. The church gradually filled with people, but he did not see Liza among them. Mass began, the deacon read the Gospel, the bell sounded for the final prayer. Lavretsky advanced a few steps, and suddenly he caught sight of Liza. She had come in before him, but he had not observed her till now. Standing in the space between the wall and the choir, to which she had pressed as close as possible, she never once looked round, never moved from her place. Lavretsky did not take his eyes off her till the service was quite finished; he was bidding her a last farewell. The congregation began to disperse, but she remained standing there. She seemed to be waiting for Lavretsky to go away. At last, however, she crossed herself for the last time, and went out without turning round. No one but a maid-servant was with her.

Lavretsky followed her out of the church, and came up with her in the street. She was walking very fast, her head drooping, her veil pulled low over her face.

"Good-day, Lizaveta Mikhailovna," he said in a loud voice, with feigned indifference. "May I accompany you?"

She made no reply. He walked on by her side.

"Are you satisfied with me?" he asked, lowering his voice. "You have heard what took place yesterday, I suppose?"

"Yes, yes," she answered in a whisper; "that was very good;" and she quickened her pace.

"Then you are satisfied?"

Liza only made a sign of assent.

"Fedor Ivanovich," she began, presently, in a calm but feeble voice, "I wanted to ask you something. Do not come any more to our house. Go away soon. We may see each other by-and-by—some day or other—a year hence, perhaps. But now, do this for my sake. In God's name, I beseech you, do what I ask!"

"I am ready to obey you in every thing, Lizaveta Mikhailovna. But can it be that we must part thus? Is it possible that you will not say a single word to me?"

"Fedor Ivanovich, you are walking here by my side. But you are already so far, far away from me; and not only you, but—"

"Go on, I entreat you!" exclaimed Lavretsky. "What do you mean?"

"You will hear, perhaps—But whatever it may be, forget— No, do not forget me—remember me."

"I forget you?"

"Enough. Farewell. Please do not follow me."

"Liza—" began Lavretsky.

"Farewell, farewell!" she repeated, and then, drawing her veil still lower over her face, she went away, almost at a run.

Lavretsky looked after her for a time, and then walked down the street with drooping head. Presently he ran against Lemm, who also was walking along with his hat pulled low over his brows, and his eyes fixed on his feet.

They looked at each other for a time in silence.

"Well, what have you to say?" asked Lavretsky at last.

"What have I to say?" replied Lemm, in a surly voice. "I have nothing to say. 'All is dead and we are dead.' (*'Alles ist todt und wir sind todt.'*) Do you go to the right?"

"Yes."

"And I am going to the left. Good-bye."

*　*　*　*　*

On the following morning Lavretsky took his wife to Lavriki. She went in front in a carriage with Ada and Justine. He followed behind in a tarantass. During the whole time of the journey, the little girl never stirred from the carriage-window. Every thing astonished her: the peasant men and women, the cottages, the wells, the arches over the horses' necks, the little bells hanging from them, and the numbers of rooks. Justine shared her astonishment. Varvara Pavlovna kept laughing at their remarks and exclamations. She was in excellent spirits; she had had an explanation with her husband before leaving O.

"I understand your position," she had said to him; and, from the expression of her quick eyes, he could see that she did completely understand his position. "But you will do me at least this justice—you will allow that I am an easy person to live with. I shall not obtrude myself on you, or annoy you. I only wished to ensure Ada's future; I want nothing more."

"Yes, you have attained all your ends," said Lavretsky.

"There is only one thing I dream of now; to bury myself for ever in seclusion. But I shall always remember your kindness—"

"There! enough of that!" said he, trying to stop her.

"And I shall know how to respect your tranquillity and your independence," she continued, bringing her preconcerted speech to a close.

Lavretsky bowed low. Varvara understood that her husband silently thanked her.

The next day they arrived at Lavriki towards evening. A week later Lavretsky went away to Moscow, having left five thousand roubles at his wife's disposal; and the day after Lavretsky's departure, Panshine appeared, whom Varvara Pavlovna had entreated not to forget her in her solitude. She received him in the most cordial manner; and, till late that night, the lofty rooms of the mansion and the very garden itself were enlivened by the sounds of music, and of song, and of joyous French talk. Panshine spent three days with

Varvara Pavlovna. When saying farewell to her, and warmly pressing her beautiful hands, he promised to return very soon—and he kept his word.

XLIII

Liza had a little room of her own on the second floor of her mother's house, a bright, tidy room, with a bedstead with white curtains in it, a small writing-table, several flower-pots in the corners and in front of the windows, and fixed against the wall a set of bookshelves and a crucifix. It was called the nursery; Liza had been born in it.

After coming back from the church where Lavretsky had seen her, she set all her things in order with even more than usual care, dusted every thing, examined all her papers and letters from her friends, and tied them up with pieces of ribbon, shut up all her drawers, and watered her flowers, giving each flower a caressing touch. And all this she did deliberately, quietly, with a kind of sweet and tranquil earnestness in the expression of her face. At last she stopped still in the middle of the room and looked slowly around her; then she approached the table over which hung the crucifix, fell on her knees, laid her head on her clasped hands, and remained for some time motionless. Presently Marfa Timofeevna entered the room and found her in that position. Liza did not perceive her arrival. The old lady went out of the room on tiptoe, and coughed loudly several times outside the door. Liza hastily rose and wiped her eyes, which shone, with gathered but not fallen tears.

"So I see you have arranged your little cell afresh," said Marfa Timofeevna, bending low over a young rose-tree in one of the flower-pots. "How sweet this smells!"

Liza looked at her aunt with a meditative air.

"What was that word you used?" she whispered.

"What word—what?" sharply replied the old lady. "It is dreadful," she continued, suddenly pulling off her cap and sitting down on Liza's bed. "It is more than I can bear. This is the fourth day I've been just as if I were boiling in a cauldron. I cannot any longer pretend I don't observe any thing. I cannot bear to see you crying, to see how pale and withered you are growing. I cannot—I cannot."

"But what makes you say that aunt?" said Liza. "There is nothing the matter with me, I—"

"Nothing?" exclaimed Marfa Timofeevna. "Tell that to some one else, not to me! Nothing! But who was on her knees just now? Whose eyelashes are still wet with tears? Nothing! Why, just look at yourself, what have you done to your face? where are your eyes gone? Nothing, indeed! As if I didn't know all!"

"Give me a little time, aunt. All this will pass away."

"Will pass away! Yes, but when? Good heavens! is it possible you have loved him so much? Why, he is quite an old fellow, Lizochka! Well, well! I don't deny he is a good man; will not bite; but what of that? We are all good people; the world isn't shut up in a corner, there will always be plenty of this sort of goodness."

"I can assure you all this will pass away—all this has already passed away."

"Listen to what I am going to tell you, Lizochka," suddenly said Marfa Timofeevna, making Liza sit down beside her on the bed, smoothing down the girl's hair, and setting her neckerchief straight while she spoke. "It seems to you, in the heat of the moment, as if it were impossible for your wound to be cured. Ah, my love, it is only death for which there is no cure. Only say to yourself, 'I won't give in—so much for him!' and you will be surprised yourself to see how well and how quickly it will all pass away. Only have a little patience."

"Aunt," replied Liza, "it has already passed away. All has passed away."

"Passed away! how passed away? Why your nose has actually grown peaky, and yet you say—'passed away.' Passed away indeed!"

"Yes, passed away, aunt—if only you are willing to help me," said Liza, with unexpected animation, and then threw her arms round Marfa Timofeevna's neck. "Dearest aunt, do be a friend to me, do help me, don't be angry with me, try to understand me—"

"But what is all this, what is all this, my mother? Don't frighten me, please. I shall cry out in another minute. Don't look at me like that: quick, tell me what is the meaning of all this!"

"I—I want—" Here Liza hid her face on Marfa Timofeevna's breast. "I want to go into a convent," she said in a low tone.

The old lady fairly bounded off the bed.

"Cross yourself, Lizochka! gather your senses together! what ever are you about? Heaven help you!" at last she stammered out. "Lie down and sleep a little, my darling. And this comes of your want of sleep, dearest."

Liza raised her head; her cheeks glowed.

"No, aunt," she said, "do not say that. I have prayed, I have asked God's advice, and I have made up my mind. All is over. My life with you here is ended. Such lessons are not given to us without a purpose; besides, it is not for the first time that I think of it now. Happiness was not for me. Even when I did indulge in hopes of happiness, my heart shuddered within me. I know all, both my sins and those of others, and how papa made our money. I know all, and all that I must pray away, must pray away. I grieve to leave you, I grieve for mamma and for Lenochka; but there is no help for it. I feel that it is impossible for me to live here longer. I have already taken leave of every thing, I have greeted every thing in the house for the last time. Something calls me away. I am sad at heart, and I would fain hide myself away for ever. Please don't hinder me or try to dissuade me; but do help me, or I shall have to go away by myself."

Marfa Timofeevna listened to her niece with horror.

"She is ill," she thought. "She is raving. We must send for a doctor; but for whom? Gedeonovsky praised some one the other day; but then he always lies—but perhaps he has actually told the truth this time."

But when she had become convinced that Liza was not ill, and was not raving—when to all her objections Liza had constantly made the same reply, Marfa Timofeevna was thoroughly alarmed, and became exceedingly sorrowful.

"But surely you don't know, my darling, what sort of life they lead in convents!" thus she began, in hopes of dissuading her. "Why they will feed you on yellow hemp oil, my own; they will dress you in coarse, very coarse clothing; they will make you go out in the cold; you will never be able to bear all this Lizochka. All these ideas of yours are Agafia's doing. It is she who has driven you out of your senses. But then she began with living, and with living to her own satisfaction. Why shouldn't you live too? At all events, let me die in peace, and then do as you please. And who on earth has ever known any one go into a convent for the sake of such-a-one—for a goat's beard—God forgive me—for a man! Why, if you're so sad at heart, you should pay a visit to a convent, pray to a saint, order prayers to be said, but don't put the black veil on your head, my *batyushka*, my *matyushka*."

And Marfa Timofeevna cried bitterly.

Liza tried to console her, wiped the tears from her eyes, and cried herself, but maintained her purpose unshaken. In her despair, Marfa Timofeevna tried to turn threats to account, said she would reveal every thing to Liza's mother; but that too had no effect. All that Liza would consent to do in consequence of the old lady's urgent entreaties, was to put off the execution of her plan for a half year. In return Marfa Timofeevna was obliged to promise that, if Liza had not changed her mind at the end of the six months, she would herself assist in the matter, and would contrive to obtain Madame Kalitine's consent.

* * * * *

As soon as the first cold weather arrived, in spite of her promise to bury herself in seclusion, Varvara Pavlovna, who had provided herself with sufficient funds, migrated to St.

Petersburg. A modest, but pretty set of rooms had been found for her there by Panshine, who had left the province of O. rather earlier than she did. During the latter part of his stay in O., he had completely lost Madame Kalitine's good graces. He had suddenly given up visiting her, and indeed scarcely stirred away from Lavriki. Varvara Pavlovna had enslaved—literally enslaved him. No other word can express the unbounded extent of the despotic sway she exercised over him.

Lavretsky spent the winter in Moscow. In the spring of the ensuing year the news reached him that Liza had taken the veil in the B. convent, in one of the most remote districts of Russia.

EPILOGUE

Eight years passed away. The spring had come again—

But we will first of all say a few words about the fate of Mikhalevich, Panshine, and Madame Lavretsky, and then take leave of them forever.

Mikhalevich, after much wandering to and fro, at last hit upon the business he was fitted for, and obtained the post of Head Inspector in one of the Government Educational Institutes. His lot thoroughly satisfies him, and his pupils "adore" him, though at the same time they mimic him. Panshine has advanced high in the service, and already aims at becoming the head of a department. He stoops a little as he walks; it must be the weight of the Vladimir Cross which hangs from his neck, that bends him forward. In him the official decidedly preponderates over the artist now. His face, though still quite young, has grown yellow, his hair is thinner than it used to be, and he neither sings nor draws any longer. But he secretly occupies himself with literature. He has written a little comedy in the style of a "proverb;" and—as every one who writes now constantly brings on the stage some real person or some actual fact—he has introduced a coquette into it, and he reads it confidentially to a few ladies who are very kind to him. But he has never married, although he has had many excellent opportunities for doing so. For that Varvara Pavlovna is to blame.

As for her, she constantly inhabits Paris, just as she used to do. Lavretsky has opened a private account for her with his banker, and has paid a sufficient sum to ensure his being free from her—free from the possibility of being a second time unexpectedly visited by her. She has grown older and stouter, but she is still undoubtedly handsome, and always dresses in taste. Every one has his ideal. Varvara Pavlovna has found hers—in the plays of M. Dumas *fils*. She assiduously frequents the theatres in which consumptive and sentimental Camelias appear on the boards; to be Madame Doche seems to her the height of human happiness. She once announced that she could not wish her daughter a happier fate. It may, however, be expected that destiny will save Mademoiselle Ada from that kind of happiness. From being a chubby, rosy child, she has changed into a pale, weak-chested girl, and her nerves are already unstrung. The number of Varvara Pavlovna's admirers has diminished, but they have not disappeared. Some of them she will, in all probability, retain to the end of her days. The most ardent of them in recent times has been a certain Zakurdalo-Skubyrnikof, a retired officer of the guard, a man of about thirty-eight years of age, wearing long mustaches, and possessing a singularly vigorous frame. The Frenchmen who frequent Madame Lavretsky's drawing-room call him *le gros taureau de l'Ukraine*. Varvara Pavlovna never invites him to her fashionable parties, but he is in full possession of her good graces.

And so—eight years had passed away. Again spring shone from heaven in radiant happiness. Again it smiled on earth and on man. Again, beneath its caress, all things began to love, to flower, to sing.

The town of O. had changed but little in the course of these

Ivan S. Turgenev

eight years, but Madame Kalitine's house had, as it were, grown young again. Its freshly-painted walls shone with a welcome whiteness, while the panes of its open windows flashed ruddy to the setting sun. Out of these windows there flowed into the street mirthful sounds of ringing youthful voices, of never-ceasing laughter. All the house seemed teeming with life and overflowing with irrepressible merriment. As for the former mistress of the house, she had been laid in the grave long ago. Maria Dmitrievna died two years after Liza took the veil. Nor did Marfa Timofeevna long survive her niece; they rest side by side in the cemetery of the town. Nastasia Carpovna also was no longer alive. During the course of several years the faithful old lady used to go every day to pray at her friend's grave. Then her time came, and her bones also were laid in the mould.

But Maria Dmitrievna's house did not pass into the hands of strangers, did not go out of her family—the nest was not torn to pieces. Lenochka, who had grown into a pretty and graceful girl; her betrothed, a flaxen locked officer of hussars; Maria Dmitrievna's son, who had only recently married at St. Petersburg, and had now arrived with his young bride to spend the spring in O.; his wife's sister, a sixteen-year-old Institute-girl, with clear eyes and rosy cheeks; and Shurochka, who had also grown up and turned out pretty—these were the young people who made the walls of the Kalitine house resound with laughter and with talk. Every thing was altered in the house, every thing had been made to harmonize with its new inhabitants. Beardless young servant-lads, full of fun and laughter, had replaced the grave old domestics of former days. A couple of setters tore wildly about and jumped upon the couches, in the rooms up and down which Roska, after it had grown fat, used to waddle seriously. In the stable many horses were stalled—clean-limbed canterers, smart trotters for the centre of the *troika*, fiery gallopers with platted manes for the side places, riding horses from the Don. The hours for breakfast, dinner, and supper, were all mixed up and confounded together. In the words of neighbors, "Such a state of things as never had been known before" had taken place.

On the evening of which we are about to speak, the inmates of the Kalitine house, of whom the eldest, Lenochka's betrothed, was not more than four-and-twenty, had taken to playing a game which was not of a very complicated nature, but which seemed to be very amusing to them, to judge by their happy laughter,—that of running about the rooms, and trying to catch each other. The dogs, too, ran about and barked; and the canaries which hung up in cages before the windows, straining their throats in rivalry, heightened the general uproar by the piercing accents of their shrill singing. Just as this deafening amusement had reached its climax, a tarantass, all splashed with mud, drew up at the front gate, and a man about forty-five years old, wearing a travelling dress, got out of it and remained standing as if bewildered.

For some time he stood at the gate without moving, but gazing at the house with observant eyes; then he entered the court-yard by the wicket-gate, and slowly mounted the steps. He encountered no one in the vestibule; but suddenly the drawing-room door was flung open, and Shurochka, all rosy red, came running out of the room; and directly afterwards, with shrill cries, the whole of the youthful band rushed after her. Suddenly, at the sight of an unknown stranger, they stopped short, and became silent; but the bright eyes which were fixed on him still retained their friendly expression, the fresh young faces did not cease to smile. Then Maria Dmitrievna's son approached the visitor, and politely asked what he could do for him.

"I am Lavretsky," said the stranger.

A friendly cry of greeting answered him—not that all those young people were inordinately delighted at the arrival of a distant and almost forgotten relative, but simply because they were ready to rejoice and make a noise over every pleasurable occurrence. They all immediately surrounded Lavretsky. Lenochka, as his old acquaintance, was the first to name herself, assuring him that, if she had had a very little more time, she would most certainly have recognized him; and then she introduced all the rest of the company to him, giving them all, her betrothed included, their familiar forms of name. The whole party then went through the dining-room into the drawing-room. The paper on the walls of both rooms had been altered, but the furniture remained just as it used to be. Lavretsky recognized the piano. Even the embroidery-frame by the window remained exactly as it had been, and in the very same position as of old; and even seemed to have the same unfinished piece of work on it which had been there eight years before. They placed him in a large arm-chair, and sat down gravely around him. Questions, exclamations, anecdotes, followed swiftly one after another.

"What a long time it is since we saw you last!" naively remarked Lenochka; "and we haven't seen Varvara Pavlovna either."

"No wonder!" her brother hastily interrupted her—"I took you away to St. Petersburg; but Fedor Ivanovich has lived all the time on his estate."

"Yes, and mamma too is dead, since then."

"And Marfa Timofeevna," said Shurochka.

"And Nastasia Corpovna," continued Lenochka, "and Monsieur Lemm."

"What? is Lemm dead too?" asked Lavretsky.

"Yes," answered young Kalitine. "He went away from here to Odessa. Some one is said to have persuaded him to go there, and there he died."

"You don't happen to know if he left any music behind?"

"I don't know, but I should scarcely think so."

A general silence ensued, and each one of the party looked at the others. A shade of sadness swept over all the youthful faces.

"But Matros is alive," suddenly cried Lenochka.

"And Gedeonovsky is alive," added her brother.

The name of Gedeonovsky at once called forth a merry laugh.

"Yes, he is still alive; and he tells stories just as he used to do," continued the young Kalitine—"only fancy! this madcap here" (pointing to his wife's sister the Institute-girl) "put a quantity of pepper into his snuff-box yesterday."

"How he did sneeze!" exclaimed Lenochka—and irrepressible laughter again broke out on all sides.

"We had news of Liza the other day," said young Kalitine. And again silence fell upon all the circle. "She is going on well—her health is gradually being restored now."

"Is she still in the same convent?" Lavretsky asked, not without an effort.

"Yes."

"Does she ever write to you?"

"No, never. We get news of her from other quarters."

A profound silence suddenly ensued. "An angel has noiselessly flown past," they all thought.

"Won't you go into the garden?" said Kalitine, addressing Lavretsky. "It is very pleasant now, although we have neglected it a little."

Lavretsky went into the garden, and the first thing he saw there was that very bench on which he and Liza had once passed a few happy moments—moments that never repeated themselves. It had grown black and warped, but still he recognized it, and that feeling took possession of his heart which is unequalled as well for sweetness as for bitterness— the feeling of lively regret, for vanished youth, for once familiar happiness.

He walked by the side of the young people along the alleys. The lime-trees looked older than before, having grown a little taller during the last eight years, and casting a denser shade. All the underwood, also, had grown higher, and the raspberry-bushes had spread vigorously, and the hazel copse was thickly tangled. From every side exhaled a fresh odor from the forest and the wood, from the grass and the lilacs.

"What a capital place for a game at Puss in the Corner!" suddenly cried Lenochka, as they entered upon a small grassy lawn surrounded by lime-trees. "There are just five of us."

"But have you forgotten Fedor Ivanovich?" asked her brother; "or is it yourself you have not counted?"

Lenochka blushed a little.

"But would Fedor Ivanovich like—at his age—" she began stammering.

"Please play away," hastily interposed Lavretsky; "don't pay any attention to me. I shall feel more comfortable if I know I am not boring you. And there is no necessity for your finding me something to do. We old people have a resource which you don't know yet, and which is better than any amusement—recollection."

The young people listened to Lavretsky with respectful, though slightly humorous politeness, just as if they were listening to a teacher who was reading them a lesson—then they all suddenly left him, and ran off to the lawn. One of them stood in the middle, the others occupied the four corners by the trees, and the game began.

But Lavretsky returned to the house, went into the dining-room, approached the piano, and touched one of the notes. It responded with a faint but clear sound, and a shudder thrilled his heart within him. With that note began the inspired melody, by means of which, on that most happy night long ago, Lemm, the dead Lemm, had thrown him into such raptures. Then Lavretsky passed into the drawing-room, and did not leave it for a long time.

In that room, in which he had seen Liza so often, her image floated more distinctly before him; the traces of her presence seemed to make themselves felt around him there. But his sorrow for her loss became painful and crushing; it bore with it none of the tranquillity which death inspires. Liza was still living somewhere, far away and lost to sight. He thought of her as he had known her in actual life; he could not recognize the girl he used to love in that pale, dim, ghostly form, half-hidden in a nun's dark robe, and surrounded by waving clouds of incense.

Nor would Lavretsky have been able to recognize himself, if he could have looked at himself as he in fancy was looking at Liza. In the course of those eight years his life had attained its final crisis—that crisis which many people never experience, but without which no man can be sure of maintaining his principles firm to the last. He had really given up thinking about his own happiness, about what would conduce to his own interests. He had become calm, and—why should we conceal the truth?—he had aged; and that not in face alone or frame, but he had aged in mind; for, indeed, not only is it difficult, but it is even hazardous to do what some people speak of—to preserve the heart young in bodily old age. Contentment, in old age, is deserved by him alone who has not lost his faith in what is good, his persevering strength of will, his desire for active employment. And Lavretsky did deserve to be contented; he had really become a good landlord; he had really learnt how to till the soil; and in that he labored, he labored not for himself alone, but he had, as far as in him lay the power, assured, and obtained guarantees for, the welfare of the peasantry on his estates.

Lavretsky went out of the house into the garden, and sat down on the bench he knew so well. There—on that loved spot, in sight of that house in which he had fruitlessly, and for the last time, stretched forth his hands towards that cup of promise in which foamed and sparkled the golden wine of enjoyment,—he, a lonely, homeless wanderer, while the joyous cries of that younger generation which had already forgotten him came flying to his ears, gazed steadily at his past life.

His heart became very sorrowful, but it was free now from

any crushing sense of pain. He had nothing to be ashamed of; he had many sources of consolation. "Play on, young vigorous lives!" he thought—and his thoughts had no taint of bitterness in them—"the future awaits you, and your path of life in it will be comparatively easy for you. You will not be obliged, as we were, to seek out your path, to struggle, to fall, to rise again in utter darkness. We had to seek painfully by what means we might hold out to the end—and how many there were amongst us who did not hold out!—but your part is now to act, to work—and the blessing of old men like me shall be with you. For my part, after the day I have spent here, after the emotions I have here experienced, nothing remains for me but to bid you a last farewell; and, although sadly, yet without a tinge of envy, without a single gloomy feeling, to say, in sight of death, in sight of my awaiting God, 'Hail, lonely old age! Useless life, burn yourself out!'"

Lavretsky rose up quietly, and quietly went away. No one observed him, no one prevented him from going. Louder than ever sounded the joyous cries in the garden, behind the thick green walls of the lofty lime-trees. Lavretsky got into his tarantass, and told his coachman to drive him home without hurrying the horses.

*   *   *   *   *

"And is that the end?" the unsatisfied reader may perhaps ask. "What became of Lavretsky afterwards? and of Liza?" But what can one say about people who are still alive, but who have already quitted the worldly stage? Why should we turn back to them? It is said that Lavretsky has visited the distant convent in which Liza has hidden herself—and has seen her. As she crossed from choir to choir, she passed close by him—passed onwards steadily, with the quick but silent step of a nun, and did not look at him. Only an almost

     Ivan S. Turgenev

imperceptible tremor was seen to move the eyelashes of the eye which was visible to him; only still lower did she bend her emaciated face; and the fingers of her clasped hands, enlaced with her rosary, still more closely compressed each other.

Of what did they both think? what did they both feel? Who can know? who shall tell? Life has its moments—has its feelings—to which we may be allowed to allude, but on which it is not good to dwell.

THE END

ABOUT THE AUTHOR

Ivan Sergeyevich Turgenev (November 9 [O.S. October 28] 1818 – September 3 [O.S. August 22] 1883) was a great Russian novelist and playwright. His novel Fathers and Sons is regarded as one of major works of 19th-century fiction.

Turgenev was born into a landed and wealthy family in Oryol, Russia, on October 28, 1818. His father Sergei Nikolaevich Turgenev, a colonel in the Imperial Russian cavalry, died when Ivan was sixteen, leaving Turgenev and his brother Nicholas to be brought up by their abusive mother, Varvara Petrovna Lutovinova. After the standard schooling for a child of a gentleman's family, Turgenev studied for one year at the University of Moscow and then moved to the University of St Petersburg, focusing on the classics, Russian literature and philology. He was sent in 1838 to the University of Berlin to study philosophy (particularly Hegel) and history.

Turgenev first made his name with A Sportsman's Sketches, also known as Sketches From a Hunter's Album or Notes of a Hunter. Based on the author's own observations while hunting birds and hares in his mother's estate of Spasskoye, the work appeared in a collected form in 1852.

In the early 1850s Turgenev wrote several short novels (povesti in Russian). In 1854 he settled in Europe and during the next year produced his first post-Russian important work: the novel "Rudin".

Choose from Thousands of 1stWorldLibrary Classics By

A. M. Barnard
Ada Leverson
Adolphus William Ward
Aesop
Agatha Christie
Alexander Aaronsohn
Alexander Kielland
Alexandre Dumas
Alfred Gatty
Alfred Ollivant
Alice Duer Miller
Alice Turner Curtis
Alice Dunbar
Allen Chapman
Alleyne Ireland
Ambrose Bierce
Amelia E. Barr
Amory H. Bradford
Andrew Lang
Andrew McFarland Davis
Andy Adams
Angela Brazil
Anna Alice Chapin
Anna Sewell
Annie Besant
Annie Hamilton Donnell
Annie Payson Call
Annie Roe Carr
Annonaymous
Anton Chekhov
Archibald Lee Fletcher
Arnold Bennett
Arthur C. Benson
Arthur Conan Doyle
Arthur M. Winfield
Arthur Ransome
Arthur Schnitzler
Arthur Train
Atticus
B.H. Baden-Powell
B. M. Bower
B. C. Chatterjee
Baroness Emmuska Orczy
Baroness Orczy
Basil King
Bayard Taylor
Ben Macomber
Bertha Muzzy Bower
Bjornstjerne Bjornson

Booth Tarkington
Boyd Cable
Bram Stoker
C. Collodi
C. E. Orr
C. M. Ingleby
Carolyn Wells
Catherine Parr Traill
Charles A. Eastman
Charles Amory Beach
Charles Dickens
Charles Dudley Warner
Charles Farrar Browne
Charles Ives
Charles Kingsley
Charles Klein
Charles Hanson Towne
Charles Lathrop Pack
Charles Romyn Dake
Charles Whibley
Charles Willing Beale
Charlotte M. Braeme
Charlotte M. Yonge
Charlotte Perkins Stetson
Clair W. Hayes
Clarence Day Jr.
Clarence E. Mulford
Clemence Housman
Confucius
Coningsby Dawson
Cornelis DeWitt Wilcox
Cyril Burleigh
D. H. Lawrence
Daniel Defoe
David Garnett
Dinah Craik
Don Carlos Janes
Donald Keyhoe
Dorothy Kilner
Dougan Clark
Douglas Fairbanks
E. Nesbit
E. P. Roe
E. Phillips Oppenheim
E. S. Brooks
Earl Barnes
Edgar Rice Burroughs
Edith Van Dyne
Edith Wharton

Edward Everett Hale
Edward J. O'Biren
Edward S. Ellis
Edwin L. Arnold
Eleanor Atkins
Eleanor Hallowell Abbott
Eliot Gregory
Elizabeth Gaskell
Elizabeth McCracken
Elizabeth Von Arnim
Ellem Key
Emerson Hough
Emilie F. Carlen
Emily Bronte
Emily Dickinson
Enid Bagnold
Enilor Macartney Lane
Erasmus W. Jones
Ernie Howard Pie
Ethel May Dell
Ethel Turner
Ethel Watts Mumford
Eugene Sue
Eugenie Foa
Eugene Wood
Eustace Hale Ball
Evelyn Everett-green
Everard Cotes
F. H. Cheley
F. J. Cross
F. Marion Crawford
Fannie E. Newberry
Federick Austin Ogg
Ferdinand Ossendowski
Fergus Hume
Florence A. Kilpatrick
Fremont B. Deering
Francis Bacon
Francis Darwin
Frances Hodgson Burnett
Frances Parkinson Keyes
Frank Gee Patchin
Frank Harris
Frank Jewett Mather
Frank L. Packard
Frank V. Webster
Frederic Stewart Isham
Frederick Trevor Hill
Frederick Winslow Taylor

Friedrich Kerst
Friedrich Nietzsche
Fyodor Dostoyevsky
G.A. Henty
G.K. Chesterton
Gabrielle E. Jackson
Garrett P. Serviss
Gaston Leroux
George A. Warren
George Ade
Geroge Bernard Shaw
George Cary Eggleston
George Durston
George Ebers
George Eliot
George Gissing
George MacDonald
George Meredith
George Orwell
George Sylvester Viereck
George Tucker
George W. Cable
George Wharton James
Gertrude Atherton
Gordon Casserly
Grace E. King
Grace Gallatin
Grace Greenwood
Grant Allen
Guillermo A. Sherwell
Gulielma Zollinger
Gustav Flaubert
H. A. Cody
H. B. Irving
H. C. Bailey
H. G. Wells
H. H. Munro
H. Irving Hancock
H. R. Naylor
H. Rider Haggard
H. W. C. Davis
Haldeman Julius
Hall Caine
Hamilton Wright Mabie
Hans Christian Andersen
Harold Avery
Harold McGrath
Harriet Beecher Stowe
Harry Castlemon
Harry Coghill
Harry Houidini

Hayden Carruth
Helent Hunt Jackson
Helen Nicolay
Hendrik Conscience
Hendy David Thoreau
Henri Barbusse
Henrik Ibsen
Henry Adams
Henry Ford
Henry Frost
Henry James
Henry Jones Ford
Henry Seton Merriman
Henry W Longfellow
Herbert A. Giles
Herbert Carter
Herbert N. Casson
Herman Hesse
Hildegard G. Frey
Homer
Honore De Balzac
Horace B. Day
Horace Walpole
Horatio Alger Jr.
Howard Pyle
Howard R. Garis
Hugh Lofting
Hugh Walpole
Humphry Ward
Ian Maclaren
Inez Haynes Gillmore
Irving Bacheller
Isabel Cecilia Williams
Isabel Hornibrook
Israel Abrahams
Ivan Turgenev
J. G.Austin
J. Henri Fabre
J. M. Barrie
J. M. Walsh
J. Macdonald Oxley
J. R. Miller
J. S. Fletcher
J. S. Knowles
J. Storer Clouston
J. W. Duffield
Jack London
Jacob Abbott
James Allen
James Andrews
James Baldwin

James Branch Cabell
James DeMille
James Joyce
James Lane Allen
James Lane Allen
James Oliver Curwood
James Oppenheim
James Otis
James R. Driscoll
Jane Abbott
Jane Austen
Jane L. Stewart
Janet Aldridge
Jens Peter Jacobsen
Jerome K. Jerome
Jessie Graham Flower
John Buchan
John Burroughs
John Cournos
John F. Kennedy
John Gay
John Glasworthy
John Habberton
John Joy Bell
John Kendrick Bangs
John Milton
John Philip Sousa
John Taintor Foote
Jonas Lauritz Idemil Lie
Jonathan Swift
Joseph A. Altsheler
Joseph Carey
Joseph Conrad
Joseph E. Badger Jr
Joseph Hergesheimer
Joseph Jacobs
Jules Vernes
Julian Hawthrone
Julie A Lippmann
Justin Huntly McCarthy
Kakuzo Okakura
Karle Wilson Baker
Kate Chopin
Kenneth Grahame
Kenneth McGaffey
Kate Langley Bosher
Kate Langley Bosher
Katherine Cecil Thurston
Katherine Stokes
L. A. Abbot
L. T. Meade

L. Frank Baum
Latta Griswold
Laura Dent Crane
Laura Lee Hope
Laurence Housman
Lawrence Beasley
Leo Tolstoy
Leonid Andreyev
Lewis Carroll
Lewis Sperry Chafer
Lilian Bell
Lloyd Osbourne
Louis Hughes
Louis Joseph Vance
Louis Tracy
Louisa May Alcott
Lucy Fitch Perkins
Lucy Maud Montgomery
Luther Benson
Lydia Miller Middleton
Lyndon Orr
M. Corvus
M. H. Adams
Margaret E. Sangster
Margret Howth
Margaret Vandercook
Margaret W. Hungerford
Margret Penrose
Maria Edgeworth
Maria Thompson Daviess
Mariano Azuela
Marion Polk Angellotti
Mark Overton
Mark Twain
Mary Austin
Mary Catherine Crowley
Mary Cole
Mary Hastings Bradley
Mary Roberts Rinehart
Mary Rowlandson
M. Wollstonecraft Shelley
Maud Lindsay
Max Beerbohm
Myra Kelly
Nathaniel Hawthrone
Nicolo Machiavelli
O. F. Walton
Oscar Wilde

Owen Johnson
P.G. Wodehouse
Paul and Mabel Thorne
Paul G. Tomlinson
Paul Severing
Percy Brebner
Percy Keese Fitzhugh
Peter B. Kyne
Plato
Quincy Allen
R. Derby Holmes
R. L. Stevenson
R. S. Ball
Rabindranath Tagore
Rahul Alvares
Ralph Bonehill
Ralph Henry Barbour
Ralph Victor
Ralph Waldo Emmerson
Rene Descartes
Ray Cummings
Rex Beach
Rex E. Beach
Richard Harding Davis
Richard Jefferies
Richard Le Gallienne
Robert Barr
Robert Frost
Robert Gordon Anderson
Robert L. Drake
Robert Lansing
Robert Lynd
Robert Michael Ballantyne
Robert W. Chambers
Rosa Nouchette Carey
Rudyard Kipling
Saint Augustine
Samuel B. Allison
Samuel Hopkins Adams
Sarah Bernhardt
Sarah C. Hallowell
Selma Lagerlof
Sherwood Anderson
Sigmund Freud
Standish O'Grady
Stanley Weyman
Stella Benson
Stella M. Francis

Stephen Crane
Stewart Edward White
Stijn Streuvels
Swami Abhedananda
Swami Parmananda
T. S. Ackland
T. S. Arthur
The Princess Der Ling
Thomas A. Janvier
Thomas A Kempis
Thomas Anderton
Thomas Bailey Aldrich
Thomas Bulfinch
Thomas De Quincey
Thomas Dixon
Thomas H. Huxley
Thomas Hardy
Thomas More
Thornton W. Burgess
U. S. Grant
Upton Sinclair
Valentine Williams
Various Authors
Vaughan Kester
Victor Appleton
Victor G. Durham
Victoria Cross
Virginia Woolf
Wadsworth Camp
Walter Camp
Walter Scott
Washington Irving
Wilbur Lawton
Wilkie Collins
Willa Cather
Willard F. Baker
William Dean Howells
William le Queux
W. Makepeace Thackeray
William W. Walter
William Shakespeare
Winston Churchill
Yei Theodora Ozaki
Yogi Ramacharaka
Young E. Allison
Zane Grey